ONLY THE UNIVERSE KNOWS!

ONLY THE UNIVERSE KNOWS!

A Lifetime of Torment, Mysteries and Discovery: The Wendy Barnhill Story

WENDY BARNHILL

gatekeeper press

Columbus, Ohio

Only the Universe Knows: The Wendy Barnhill Story

Published by Gatekeeper Press
2167 Stringtown Rd, Suite 109
Columbus, OH 43123-2989
www.GatekeeperPress.com

ISBN (hardcover): 9781642376227

Printed in the United States of America

Dedication

This book is dedicated to my three wonderful children who have accompanied me and supported me through this incredible journey; and to my granddaughter. It is also dedicated to all those who have known similar experiences, endured similar pain and abuse, asked the same questions, and in search of the same answers

To consider the Earth as the only populated world in infinite space is as absurd as to assert that in an entire field of millet, only one grain will grow.

—*Metrodorus of Chios*

Contents

Foreword

WE ALL KNOW of the existence of dysfunction, violence and chaos in this world. We know of children who were born into that existence and the horrible consequences they endured as a result. We know that many do not survive, while those that do, frequently grow to immerse themselves in that very culture, repeating the same mistakes, living only what they were taught.

Yet, we know of others who were able to escape that culture to become healthy, functioning human beings. In many cases, they had to scratch and claw their way out. To escape, they often had to turn their backs on loved ones who embodied what they were escaping.

And that's just in this world.

Beyond the good, bad and ugly we can see and touch in this world, there are things we can only imagine and wonder about in the outer world. Are we alone? What exists beyond the world we know? Is there an existence beyond the earth and the vast universe that surrounds it? Beyond our physical and psychological powers, what are our spiritual powers? Beyond our faith, what is our true connection to those spiritual powers? Are we born with them? Are they somehow injected into our bodies? Is it possible to even experience the supernatural, much less retain some of its qualities?

We know the dismissive skepticism and ridicule those questions provoke. And we know how that skepticism intensifies if you dare offer a theory or explanation for its existence.

But for some, those outer world experiences are as real as those that occur to us here on earth.

The Wendy Barnhill Story is a convergence of those two domains . . . painful, abusive experiences from the world we know; and experiences that only pose questions about the otherworldly things we can only wonder about.

Hers is a conflagration of those things we know all too well, or may have experienced, intertwined in the mysteries of what lies beyond, in search of answers that only the universe knows.

—*G. Ross Kelly*

Introduction

M OST STORIES DO not begin with a *Warning: Read at Your Own Discretion* message the way an X-rated movie or television show might. Mine does.

It is not because my story is X-rated or pornographic in nature, but because it takes you into the realm of the ugliest form of life of this world, and into the unknown, the unbelievable, or the *I refuse to believe* category of another world.

So, if you choose to put this book down now and decide to read no further, I will understand. My story is not for the faint of heart. Nor is it for those whose reality does not allow them to venture beyond the physical world, into the land of spirituality or the world of the unknown. Further, it is not for those who seek unusual stories simply for the sake of novelty, ridicule, or mindless entertainment.

In contrast, my story is for those who may not know the spiritual realm, or the world of celestial existence, but has felt it, or wondered about it, or was genuinely curious about it.

It may never be fully resolved. Mine would be an easy story to dismiss as one of a kook or a product of the underworld who has done one too many drugs. While I may be all those things, it doesn't mean my story didn't happen. It just means it is beyond the realm of the normal human experience. My story is a mystery, which began at birth and was only partially solved in the last 10 years.

In short, my story is for the believers or those open to believing. It is for those who believe that we are not alone. It is for those who can embrace the concept of a higher power and a world beyond our own. It for those who have experienced strange or unexplained circumstances and are in search of answers. It is for those who have known difficult or unfortunate circumstances and are in search of affirmation that their misfortune was not in vein, but in the pursuit of a higher purpose.

My story will take you into the underbelly of dysfunction, violence, heartache and abuse, into a life of the unknown, and ultimately into a life of redemption. My story will take you into the outer limits of your belief system . . . a world that most people know and enjoy only through science fiction stories and movies. My story will take you into a world believed to exist only in the furtive imaginations of Walt Disney, Steven Spielberg or George Lucas . . . a world we would love to believe in but are unable to venture to the outer edges of our realities.

Mine is a life of being blessed, or cursed, depending on your perspective, at a very young age with extraordinary circumstances and an uncanny psychic ability. I have seen or experienced things that, to this day, I do not understand. It began with a strange encounter that happened to me at the tender age of seven, which can only be believed by blind faith, a lie detector test, or an intense examination. And I welcome any combination of the three.

In that initial encounter, I was thrust into a paranormal, almost celestial experience of another world and another consciousness. I was returned only to go from one bizarre event to another including experiencing my own death.

One working theory which I am still trying to unravel begins with my father.

My father's life was dark, violent and mysterious, both in his military and civilian life. He served multiple tours in Vietnam and participated in heinous behaviors that garnered headlines during that time which resulted in the prosecution of other veterans. The effects of that war ranged from exposure to chemicals and drugs to PTSD. And when he returned home, married my mother and had me, whatever he had in his DNA was passed on to me.

How, you may ask, could that be the outcome when thousands of Vietnam war veterans returned home under the same conditions? My father was not a run-of-the-mill war veteran. He was in what would be referred to as 'black ops', engaged in unspeakable activities using unspeakable devices and tactics. What he was doing was not the subject of the nightly news people watched on television during the war. It was more like the war inside the war. The Dark War.

Years later, he shared those experiences with me in ways that a child should never know. He returned with much of his war memorabilia and records, which he kept, locked away in a military locker in his home. My father forbade me from seeing the contents, but I did manage to sneak into the locker once. I saw maps of North Vietnam, photographs, and records I did not fully understand, but I understood enough to know what I was seeing was sinister and probably illegal.

When my father discovered me combing through what was obviously classified materials, he beat me and warned me that I would be in danger if it was ever discovered that I had viewed the materials. I never tried again to view the materials, but later in life, my father shared more about his undercover activities.

When he returned to civilian life from his multiple tours in Vietnam, my father's life became even darker, even more sinister as he became part of the underworld of organized crime.

For reasons that will become apparent as you read, no names will be used in telling my story, including those of my immediate and extended family members. Far beyond any legal concerns, the risks of physical harm to me and my family are very real.

In short, my life was predominantly characterized by violence, physical and sexual abuse, dysfunction and mystery. And through it all, I only wanted what everyone seeks . . . love, understanding and a sense of normalcy. But most of all, I wanted answers . . .

I know my childhood was marred in dysfunction and violence. I realize I was an inconvenience in both my Mom and Dad's life, being passed back and forth between the two of them like a bad debt. I know my childhood experiences catapulted me into an adult existence that perpetuated the very experiences I sought to escape. I know I experienced health issues that resulted in me dying on a hospital bed only to be revived.

What I don't know, however, is why those real-life experiences, as unfortunate, regretful and debilitating as they may have been, were compounded by a series of otherworld occurrences that baffle me to this day.

- *What happened that fateful night as I approached my seventh birthday, and the days that followed?*

- *What happened that day as I lay in my hospital room with no remaining visible signs of life for an extended period of time, yet could see the entire experience and aftermath outside of my own body, only to return to this life?*

- *Why do I know things about catastrophic events, from floods to volcanic eruptions around the world before they occur?*

- *Why do I see a visible glow which surrounds everyone I encounter, reflecting their energy, their intentions, and their spirit?*

- *What bestowed me, or cursed me, with those experiences, those abilities that have haunted me throughout my life? Was it my father's very DNA that shaped and influenced my fate? Or, did I inadvertently wander into these situations blindly?*

Some of these experiences may have explanations grounded in this world. Some of them, however, are clearly in the realm of the supernatural. Whatever those explanations, I remain, even today, confused, dismayed, yet determined.

Some forty years later, here I stand ... still seeking that love and understanding, as well as explanations. I possess extrasensory powers and an uncanny knowledge of the workings of our universe, but I have yet to find the simple joys and happiness here on earth. But I'm still here and my search continues.

If you dare, come with me into my world, an existence that has both haunted me and intrigued me since I was a child. Learn of my experiences, follow me on my journey, and discover my message. Perhaps you will discover that you have been there too.

This is my story.

Wendy

CHAPTER 1

The Merger from Hell

MY MOTHER NEVER had a chance . . .

From the very beginning of her life, the woman that would become my mother was searching for a way out... out of a cesspool of near-poverty, violence, abuse and disregard for human life. Her surroundings as a child were surrounded by tragedy and violence.

Hers was a childhood of sheer agony. She was subjected to unspeakable violence and brutality. She witnessed family members stabbing one another, beating one another, and even killing one another. At age seven, out of revenge, she murdered her own grandfather, then made a failed attempt to take her own life.

At the age of fifteen, she had to assume responsibility for what was a literal sewer of dysfunctional chaos. Her mother died and as the oldest sibling, she became the caretaker for her brothers and sisters. By then, however, she was making plans for her escape. She had her radar fully programmed to find the nearest exit. She wanted out.

She wanted out of her shackles to find a better life, and she wasn't very particular about what that life might look like. Whatever it was, it had to have been better than what she was used to.

The man who would become my father originally hailed from

a small town in Florida, but after returning home from Vietnam, he found himself in a bar across the state. Perhaps based on his experiences in Vietnam or perhaps based on his own childhood experiences, or both, he was a man consumed with anger, violence and mystery.

As bitter and angry as my mother had become because of her own experiences, my father was even worse. Exactly what he was doing in Vietnam, no one was quite sure. How many tours he had served in Vietnam was equally unclear. The vagaries were plenty. He always had secrets. Was he still in the military? Was he still associated with the military in some form and dispatched to the area where he was living? Or, was he discharged and now a civilian?

Nobody was quite sure. Everything about his past was on a strict 'need to know' basis, and anyone who dared to inquire incurred his wrath. All that was really known about my father was that he had a former wife and son in the area; and that he was an angry, violent man. I later learned he left behind another child in Vietnam. Before my mom and dad ever met, I would have two half-siblings I would never know.

When they did meet, they were two powder kegs looking for a match.

Their initial encounter took place in 1971 in that bar. My mom was in search of a white knight. My dad was in search of a cure for a lonely night. Once he bought her a drink, their fate, and mine, were set for life. One drink led to another, and then another. As the drinks flowed, they started looking better and better to each other. Somewhere along the way, drinks led to an alcohol-induced tryst in a back room, or a back alley, or a back seat, or somewhere, and I was conceived.

After that fateful night, they could barely remember each other's name, but that didn't stop them from getting married.

There is an expression that when one homeless person hooks up with another homeless person, they are still homeless. The parallel is when one angry, bitter, twisted individual hooks up with another, that anger and bitterness becomes magnified.

Two people don't magically change when they get married. Whomever they were before they married each other is who they are after they are wed, now only now living in the confined same space. It was like putting a wildcat and a bulldog in the same pen and being surprised when they attack each other.

The anger, violence and dysfunction that defined their lives as individuals was now compressed into an 1800 square foot house, or trailer to be exact. They set up house in a trailer park in the area and brought their baggage with them, literally and figuratively.

With the bitterness and rage imprinted upon her during her home life, my mother thought she may have found the answer to her desperate search for a better life. Instead, what she found was simply an intensified strain of that violence, anger and dysfunction.

It is from that merger from hell that I became an inconvenient by-product some nine months later.

CHAPTER 2

Born Under a Bad Sign

MY DADDY WAS born came from some pretty interesting lineage, including a famous actor I cannot reveal and a member of some well-known families. There was a violent streak in my daddy's family, and that strain certainly rubbed off on him. He learned early in life that nothing was given, and whatever you want in this life you must take it, no matter the means and no matter who it might hurt. He had two means of communicating . . . violence and rage.

My mother, who was born in Florida, had a rough go of it from the very beginning. She was deemed to be very smart but whatever opportunities she had to apply that intelligence were stolen by a combination of her circumstances and bad choices. Her mother died when she was a mere teenager, leaving her to assume that role for her siblings. By the time she met my daddy, she had already gone through one marriage, and would go through more before it was all said and done.

I was born in June of 1972. Neither of my parents were prepared, nor even interested in raising a baby. I was like a child being raised by two children on crack cocaine. Individually, each of them had talent, intelligence, and loads of potential. But together, they were like dynamite and matches. Their marriage was a mixture of passion, alcohol, violence, abuse and mystery, and my presence was an inconvenience for both of them.

By the time I was born my mama and daddy had settled into a routine that was anything but routine. As best we know, my father had a job as a truck driver that took him on long extended absences for days and sometimes weeks at a time. I learned later that his job was in part legitimate, and in part a front for his other activities that we were not supposed to know about. My mother rarely saw him, and at times, had no idea where he was.

I don't know if he was present for my birth, or he was somewhere on one of his mysterious trips. If he was there for my birth, it wouldn't be long until he was on the road again. I'm surprised they even chose to have me. They certainly weren't prepared to take care of me.

Violence came naturally in my house. My parents didn't just argue . . . they *fought,* physically. As a child, I remember assuming every married couple's arguments turned physical, and I assumed every child was beaten when they did something wrong. And I don't mean just whipped with a belt or spanked. I mean *beaten.*

Having a baby in the house to my parents was the equivalent of having dirty clothes lying on the floor, or garbage that needed to be taken out. At best, I was an afterthought. Mostly, I was an inconvenience . . . an inconvenience with a bad attitude.

Unfortunately, the two of them were my early role models. As they argued, I learned to argue. As they settled an argument by screaming and fighting, I learned to do the same. At a very early age, I was left to fend for myself. If I was going to survive, I had to learn to speak up. And more times than not, in my father's eyes, that was interpreted as talking back, which led to being beaten.

My father didn't know how to discipline . . . he only knew how to punish! He exacted the same brutality on a two-year old child, as he would a thirty-year-old man in a bar fight. Corporal punishment, for me, was getting a violent beating.

I had what my Daddy called a smart mouth. Little did he realize, I was simply mimicking him.

By the time I was three years old I was already learning about the ugly side of life. My parents had separated and me and my mom were living with my grandparents. I was usually pawned off to a babysitter who had begun to sexually abuse me. Did I mention I was three?

To get away from him, one day I ran away from his house to go back my grandparents, but when I got there, I beat on the door, but no one answered. Typically, that meant they had been out drinking the night before or being at the dog track.

Eventually, I was shuttled back and forth between my mom and dad, who was always on the road and seldom home. That meant I was shuttled around to anyone who would watch me at the time. Which many times, resulted in more abuse.

As childhoods go, mine was clearly off to a rocky beginning. Between the tumultuous state of my parents' on again, off again relationship, and me being passed around and sexually abused, my earliest memories are painful ones.

I was living in a sea of turmoil, violence and bedlam with no parental guidance. But through it all, I learned quickly how to survive and developed an abiding faith in the process.

Fortunately, I was also smart.

By the time I was three, I had learned to read and write. I'm not sure how it happened, but learning seemed to come easy to me. It was probably my survival instinct protecting me from whatever may be happening in the next room. By the time I was two, I could say my ABC's and count to fifty. By the time I was three, I was reading bedtime stories to myself.

I was smart and self-sufficient at an early age, but it didn't come from any type of training or grooming . . . it came out of sheer animalistic survival. My childhood training was not how to be proper and well-mannered; it more like the laws of the jungle . . . survival of the fittest. If you saw something you wanted, you took it, whether it was yours or not. You might be punished for it later, but we lived for the moment, and that moment was all I knew.

I witnessed adult behavior no child should ever see. I remember being left alone when I yearned to be comforted, yet I would begin to tremble when I heard footsteps coming my way. I never knew what form of mistreatment or abuse accompanied those footsteps.

There was one thing I was learning that was in stark contrast to the way my parents behaved during my early childhood. Whether through my grandmother, my aunt, or some other means, I was exposed to the Bible and intrigued with the teachings of Jesus. Having taught myself to read at an early age, I found myself constantly reading the Bible.

When other preschoolers were reading about Dick and Jane and Dr. Seuss, I was reading the Bible. Perhaps that was my refuge from the bedlam that surrounded me. Perhaps it was my source of sanity amidst the sea of insanity.

Whatever it was, I developed a deep and abiding faith at a very early age, and it grew stronger as the years progressed. It would clearly be my refuge as events unfolded around me.

By the time I was seven, I was wise beyond my years. But no degree of wisdom or street smarts would prepare me for what would happen next. My faith was subjected to an early test.

CHAPTER 3

A Childhood Interrupted

WHAT WOULD BECOME the first of many strange and bizarre incidents in my life, took place as I approached my seventh birthday. I experienced what few people on this earth have ever experienced, and what even fewer are willing to talk about. Whether it was an alien abduction or just some sort of paranormal experience, I don't know. I just know that, at a very early age, I was catapulted into the world of the bizarre.

> *Two possibilities exist: Either we are alone in the universe or we are not. Both are equally terrifying.*
>
> *—Arthur C. Clarke*

My daddy was a truck driver. At least that's what he *said* he was. As I grew older, I came to believe that was just a cover for him being away from home for long stretches of time and doing whatever he was up to. But, when you are six years old, you believe anything your Daddy says.

All I really knew in those days was that he wandered in and out of my Mom's life and mine. For my Mom, her relationship with my father was a tumultuous relationship filled with turmoil and uncertainty. For me, he just seemed to be away for long stretches of time. As a result, for long periods, it was just my Mom and me at home alone. Those times were the most peaceful in our house.

When my Daddy was home, he and my Mom were usually fighting. Those were times when the household became loud and many times violent. Living in a trailer park in a small town in Florida, there were nights when the whole trailer shook. I may not have known what they were fighting about, but I was more attuned to their anger and violence than they thought I was.

A child knows when times are peaceful and when there is conflict or danger in the air. And that night, I could feel danger in the air.

My Dad had just gotten home from one of his prolonged absences and, right away, I could sense trouble brewing. I don't know if my Mom had pissed him off or what. Maybe she had questioned his whereabouts, or maybe she had burned his dinner. Whatever the issue was, he seemed to be getting madder buy the minute. The situation was heated.

Me? I was in my bedroom, which was at the far end of the trailer. In their mind, I was asleep. But to the contrary, I was far from sleeping. I was sitting up in my bed, straining to hear every word being spoken. The argument was taking place in the kitchen at the other end of our trailer. The arguing soon escalated to screaming, and the screaming became physical.

When you are seven years old, you may not understand the true nature of adult conversations, but you know when a situation is not good, and this situation was becoming increasingly not good. As best I could tell, it was around 8:30 to 9:00 o'clock in the evening.

Up to this point, as I listened to the turmoil unfolding in the kitchen, I remained huddled in my bed with my knees tucked under my chin, shaking at the unknown perils that were happening. I grew increasingly nervous and was scared by the loud noises coming from the kitchen.

As the violence escalated, rather than run in the opposite direction, I felt the urge to get closer. I don't know if it was the instinct to protect my mother, or if my curiosity simply got the best of me. Whatever it was, it drew me closer. I quietly got out of my bed and went to the doorway to better hear their arguing.

The door of my bedroom was probably the absolute limit to which I could go and remain safely out of harm's way. However, for reasons I cannot explain, rather than stay where I would be safe, I continued to venture further out of my room, and into the open hallway. I continued to inch nearer the line of fire. As I drew closer, I suddenly watched my Mom being hurled across the kitchen floor. My first instinct was to protect my mother, but I also wanted to remain silent and undetected.

Just as my mother was trying to defend herself from the next blow, my father caught a glimpse of me standing in the hallway witnessing the entire episode. Seeing me as a witness to what was going on, he immediately stopped the attack on my mother, and turned toward me. I was now his target. I was not supposed to be witnessing how he was treating my Mom. He began running down the hallway towards me. He was already taking off his belt as he approached me. I knew that belt.

Knowing what was in store for me, I ran and jumped back in my bed, and once again assumed my sitting fetal position with my knees tucked under my chin. My heart was racing, and I was rocking back and forth in my bed and began screaming for Jesus.

When my Dad arrived at my doorway, belt in hand, I knew this was not going to be an idle threat for spying on him and my Mom. He was going to beat me because of what I had witnessed. But the moment he crossed the doorway into my room, a most bizarre scenario, so unnatural that I cannot explain to this day, began to unfold.

With one foot in my doorway, and with me on my bed shivering in fear, my father froze in mid stride. I don't mean he stopped on his own accord. I mean it was as if the scene that was unfolding was on video tape, and someone pressed the 'pause' button.

The final image I had of my father that night was of him frozen in mid-stride, as if in a state of suspended animation, with one foot in my bedroom and the other in the hallway. While my father's body went into 'freeze frame' mode, the supernatural scenario continued. A sheet of blue icy flames began to erupt around my bed.

Had I reverted into some protective emotional state to insulate me from the violence I was about to incur? Had some spirit swooped in to protect me? Had some supernatural experience occurred?

In a normal situation this would be a frightening scene. But strangely, I felt no heat, nor danger from the flames; only the sensation of being engulfed in a cocoon of fire. I had no more fear of the wrath of my father. I was calm . . . no longer afraid.

That is the last thing I remember that night.

Whether I blacked out, or whether some supernatural power rendered me unconscious and took possession of my body and soul, the next twelve hours in my life remain to this day to be an absolute blank. Neither I nor anyone else to this day has been able to explain or understand what happened on that night of September 29th, 1979, my seventh birthday.

From the moment my father's body was frozen in mid-stride and my bed began was surrounded by flames, I blacked out. The next thing I know is that I was being awakened by my aunt.

It was 10:00 the following morning and when I was awakened, I was still sitting on my bed in the same locked fetal position with my knees tucked under my chin and my arms clasped tightly around my legs.

My aunt was my mother's sister and lived in the trailer across the road. I awoke to her grabbing me by the right arm, struggling to shake my arms loose from me having locked them around my legs. Finally, able to do so, she took me to her trailer across the road.

As I look back on that fateful night, I find it strange that I would be in the same fetal position, sitting upright on my bed. It seems logical that, if I had fallen asleep at some point during that night, my body would have naturally relaxed and I would have slumped into a prone, sleeping position.

How is it that, some 12 hours later, my aunt found me frozen in the same sitting position on my bed? No one has ever been able to provide a logical explanation. I was equally perplexed by what happened to my mom and dad. I was no longer a prisoner of their hysteria.

What I do know is that my aunt, or something, intervened to rescue the me from the fighting that was taking place between my Mom and Dad. My aunt knew that I had been subjected to an adult situation that no child should have to witness and was going to remove me from that situation and take me to her trailer across the road. But why the next morning? Why not that night?

And how would she have intervened to save me from the brute force and violence of my father? She would have been as vulnerable and susceptible to his rage and bullying as my mother? Or me?

Once my father crossed the threshold of my bedroom that night, the rest of the evening was a blur to me, leaving me filled with questions that remain to this day. I continue to have reoccurring nightmares and occasional flashes of that entire episode.

One minute my father was entering my bedroom with his belt in his hand preparing to beat me. The next minute, his body was in freeze frame and my bed was engulfed in a brilliant blue flame. At the time, I was not sure of what had happened. I just know that sometime the next morning, my aunt woke me and took me to her house, across the road.

I could not make sense of all that had happened that night, nor did I try to. I was a child, and as a child, I did what children do . . . move on. As the following morning progressed, though I continued to have reoccurring images of the night before, I began to drift back into my play mode.

But again, that too, would change.

Despite having endured a night filled with domestic violence and some inexplicable paranormal experience, by the following morning, I was back into being a seven-year-old girl again. Along with other friends, I went to play in a neighborhood playground area, where there was a set of monkey bars.

Those monkey bars were my favorite outdoor activity. I was on the monkey bars with my friends playing 'bats' (hanging upside down by your knees, imitating the posture of bats), when yet a second bizarre event occurred. This was less than 24 hours after the first inexplicable event had occurred.

As I was hanging upside down, I was enjoying the view of the sky and the trees, when suddenly I could hear the sound of whirring or humming, similar to the way a refrigerator or air conditioner hums. It seemed to be coming from the sky. From my upside-down position, I suddenly saw a large, bright silver metallic object that looked as big as a bus, or even a football field. It came so close to me that I instinctively tried to reach out to touch it. I reached for it but could not touch it. It continued moving in a slow straight-line direction for seconds, or even a minute.

And then, as quickly as it first appeared, it disappeared.

Before I or any of my friends had the opportunity to digest what we had just witnessed, a big, black government looking sedan drove up to the area where we were playing. Two men, both dressed in dark suits, tie and wearing hats, perfectly profiling the *Men in Black*, approached us.

Without a word to greet us, say hello to us, or boo, they began quizzing us about what we may or may not have seen.

"Did you see anything?"
"Which way did it go?'
"Can you describe it?"
"How high or how close was it to you?"

"Did anyone get out?"
"How long was it in the area?"

Strangely, they also wanted to know, *"Why were we hanging upside down. Why were we playing 'bats?"* It was if that was a strange or mysterious behavior for little girls.

They immediately began to try to convince us that we did not see what we had just seen. This was nothing out of the ordinary, they said. They explained how we were near a military installation and there are weather balloons that are frequently in the area. *That,* they said with certainty, is what we most likely saw. Feeling we were convinced of what we saw and didn't see, just as abruptly as they arrived, the two men drove off.

First, I had experienced the most bizarre incident in my life the night before when some unexplained supernatural power interceded to freeze the movements of me and my father and surround my bed with a blue flame. Secondly, on the following day, I observed some unexplained object in the sky that appeared, and then disappeared in a matter of seconds. Third, in an instant after seeing this object, I was visited by two men, whose objective seemed to be to convince me and my friend that we did not see what we saw.

I was a seven-year-old child, but I knew enough to know that whatever I saw that day, was connected to what had happened the night before. From the earliest days of my childhood, I was never an innocent little girl living any semblance of a normal life. But, given the events of the previous two days took the strange, the dark nature of my childhood had risen to a new level.

The constant physical abuse and mistreatment by my parents were now the least of my concerns.

Over the following days, I grew increasingly irritable. I could no longer sleep. I had bad dreams. I was no longer interested in school. I was becoming increasingly inquisitive and frustrated that no one could explain the events of that fateful 24-hour period. My mother

was of no help. She and everyone else dismissed my accounts . . . .
"I'm sure it was nothing". *"It was probably just your imagination."*

That span of 24 hours on September 29 and 30th in 1979, the day of my seventh birthday, would change my life forever. I was transformed from a playful, precocious, smart-mouthed seven-year-old, into a girl who had lost the final remnants of her childhood innocence. I was full of guilt, anger and turmoil.

Those two days were just the beginning of a life filled with mystery, turmoil, an obsession with the occult; and feeling rejected, disbelieved, dismissed, and terribly alone.

That combination of experiences and the bundle of emotions that followed, robbed me of my childhood before my eighth birthday, and leaving me to trust no one.

From there, my life went even deeper into the morass. I had nightmares constantly and still being molested and raped by members of my family and babysitters. A life that had begun in an environment of rage, violence and turmoil, had now truly become one of a most macabre, ghoulish hellish state.

Seemingly oblivious to what I had experienced and the turmoil I was feeling as a result, my Mom and Dad never altered their course. The anger, dysfunction and violence between them continued unabated. There were numerous occasions when the cops had to be called to intervene.

My Mom eventually left my Dad, and for a time we moved in with my aunt.

Though there was nothing but bedlam between my mother and daddy, as a little girl I held tightly to the few good moments I could remember between the three of us. I remember us taking rides around the countryside. I remember accompanying him to his hometown, where he would go hunting with his brother. I remember him taking me to Disneyworld.

On those few occasions, I was doing the things that normal little girls do with their parents. Unfortunately, those occasions were few and far between, but like all little girls, those were the memories I clung to. As bizarre as it may seem, given all I had experienced, I missed my father.

Once again single, my Mom had to rely on herself to fend for the two of us and worked a variety of odd jobs including being a bartender. And once again, on many situations, I was left to fend for myself.

The behavioral experts say that, in the absence of structure, a child makes their own. That was certainly true for me. And it was not always a good kind of structure.

My Dad was gone, but he was not completely out of our lives. There was a time when he would stalk and intimidate my Mom, at her home and where she worked. At times, he even stalked me at school. Life was not good for us. Though he was no longer with us, his violence and rage were never far away. The strange thing, however, was that as tumultuous and violent as the situation was between my Mom and Dad, I still missed my Dad.

My Mom and I continued to move around, and the strange events continued to follow. There was the time when my room was filled with scorpions, inexplicably. At one time, we moved out of the trailer park and into an old colonial era cooking house across the road. It was furnished with big thick 1920's era-looking furniture, as if it were haunted.

The bed in which I was sleeping would 'breathe.' The mattress would move up and down as if it was a human taking big, deep breaths. Still haunted by the earlier events in my life, that frightened me. I would tell my Mom how the bed was breathing, and I could not sleep in that bed. But, again, I was dismissed.

All I wanted was to be a normal little girl. Instead, I lived in the world of the macabre and in the darkest shadows of humanity. And all of it would be dismissed as if it were only my imagination.

With my parents no longer together, I kept being shuttled back and forth between the two of them, depending on who had the more compelling reason why they should not have me and the other one should.

I felt less like a daughter, and more like an inconvenience. They both had their own agendas, which seldom included me. Whatever they were up to, I seemed to always be in the way, always a continuous see-saw between the lesser of two evils.

When I was with my mother, I clearly was in the way of her own never-ending pursuits of love, for herself. After she left my father, she went through relationships like glasses of beer.

When I stayed with my father, he too, had his own agenda, and I felt equally as if I were in the way. He remained the same angry, violent man he was when he and my Mom were married. I felt his rage and abuse anytime I was with him. Yet, somehow, beyond being my Daddy, there was a strange, inexplicable magnetic pull that I would only begin to understand years later.

But it was only a matter of time before my mom would bring a new man into her life, and mine. Staying true to her nature, my Mom found a new partner. I would soon have a stepfather.

My father was now out of my mother's life and mine. Or was he? He would not go away. He was like the jilted lover that refused to leave. He still tried to exert some control over my Mom, though she had remarried. He harassed my step-father. On one occasion, he even attempted to kidnap me at school. As tumultuous as the situation was, I still missed my father.

Whatever abuse, violence, or dysfunction I may have been subjected to between my mother and my father, that was only a precursor of things to come.

CHAPTER 4

Descent into Darkness

AFTER AN EARLY childhood consumed by the weird, the violent and the paranormal, I was growing up confused, angry and in search of answers. Getting none, and worse, being dismissed as a child with an overactive imagination, I grew angrier and more rebellious. A new man was in my Mom's life, but all that meant for me was more abuse. Now, entering into my teens, I was just old enough to venture out into the world, but not yet wise enough to know better.

The results would be predictable.

When others begin to doubt you, you can either prove them wrong, or give them more evidence to feel the way the way they did.

Following that fateful 24-hour span in September of 1979, my life would never know 'normalcy' again. The remainder of my childhood and the years of my adolescence were riddled with mystery, abuse and unanswered questions, resulting in bouts of rebellion, anger, frustration and delinquency. I was growing up much too fast, knowing way too much, all while secretly yearning for the structure and guidance I so desperately needed.

I merely wanted answers. Instead, what I got was a series of misdiagnoses, drugs, and a lot of abuse, physically and sexually, and introduction to the dark underbelly of the streets.

With my parents no longer together, I continued to be bounced back and forth between the two of them, and to strangers that abused me. It was not a matter of who wanted me, but a matter of who needed me out of their situation at a particular time. Married or divorced, I was still an inconvenience that had to be dealt with.

My father's life was still shrouded in mystery and did not lend itself to having a child hanging around. My mother's life was much simpler . . . drugs and men. She was always doing drugs, marijuana mostly, and she always had a man in her life. Hers seemed to be a continuous string of relationships littered with stepsiblings and drug use.

Eventually, each of my parents were in new relationships and remarried. But, initially, neither of my new stepparents offered me anything different than the life to which I had painfully grown accustomed.

My father married a woman who was extremely possessive and jealous of any type of relationship I had with my father. My mother married a man who would eventually become the closest thing I would ever experience as a real father, but that would not happen for a long time. Our relationship had a very rocky start resulting in many more years of more turmoil and abuse.

By the time I was nine, with my Mom remarried, I thought things might get better. Her new husband also introduced into my life a slew of new stepsiblings which I looked forward to meeting and being with. Having been an only child and being the sole child and most vulnerable of abuse targets, I eagerly welcomed my new siblings.

The pattern of abuse, however, continued. I remained a victim of sexual abuse by baby sitters and total strangers.

What is it in our culture that invites the sexual abuse of a child?

I fully understand that the sexual urge is a natural one, but I also assume it to be one of discernment . . . one of choosing the right time, the right place, and the right consenting partner.

In stark contrast however, the culture in which I was living provided none of those prerequisites. It only offered more of the same, unfortunately, in greater numbers.

I was still suffering demons from my paranormal experience, whatever it was, and my new home environment was not the place to reflect on it. I was still too young to comprehend what had happened to me, and the more I tried to explain it, the more I was dismissed as a child with an overactive imagination. And, the more I was abused.

I was still haunted by the bizarre incidents that had occurred in my life, and I was still feeling their effects. By everyone's accounts, I was a bright student, but I had completely lost interest in my schoolwork. I still could not sleep and still had a difficult time concentrating. I seemed to be always agitated and ill at ease. I lashed out at people for no apparent reason.

My Mom and her new husband consulted with physicians and even mental health workers who concluded I was either bipolar, schizophrenic, or had some other mental disorder. They always attempted to remedy the situation with medication.

The more they dismissed or minimized me, the more irritated I became. I was growing increasingly frustrated and suspicious of the medical community. They seemed to have no genuine interest in what I had experienced, and their only answer was pills.

Behind his thinly veiled efforts to treat me as with some degree of love as the daughter of his new wife, my new stepdad at times demonstrated more anger than my real dad. That was further compounded by having a cadre of new brothers and sisters whom I barely knew at the time. By the time I was a teenager, my life at home was a living hell and I was looking for a way out.

Worse yet, I got no support from my mother. Her new husband forbade her from working or even getting out of the house. Her new job consisted of keeping the house clean for her demanding husband, and she didn't even do that. That job was left to me.

My mother did nothing but lay on the sofa all day and delegated her household duties to me. From scrubbing floors, to cleaning bathrooms and washing dishes, all domestic chores fell to me. And if the household was not up to my new father's expectations when he came home, I was the one who paid the price.

My stepfather, like my father, was an angry, abusive man. He not only condoned violence, he inflicted it. And he seemed to have a particular anger towards women. I was subjected to harsh punishment when he deemed it necessary, but fortunately, I will say I was not abused by him.

If the house was not perfect, he would beat me with a belt, or slap me, or even shove my face onto the floor to show me a speck of dirt that I failed to clean up. My mother was nowhere to be found in protecting or supporting me. She seemed to take pleasure in seeing me punished, viewing me as the reason she was prevented from pursuing the life she so desperately had sought.

I was a vulnerable child living in a lawless environment.

I was being physically abused by my father and sexually abused by babysitters and strangers alike and ignored by my mother. My new father told me whatever sexual abuse I was being subjected to, was my own fault. 'You *want* to be fucked,' he told me.

Yeah, I'm thirteen years old, and I *want* to be raped!

That was my new life. And my Mother stood by and let it happen. She chose to side with her new husband and stepsons, rather than her own daughter. I was left unprotected and growing increasingly angry and rebellious.

I would later learn, given her own background, combined with her drug use, she didn't know how to care for me.

CHAPTER 5

Children Having Children

A FTER THE DEATH of my grandmother, I looked for anyway I could find to escape the madness that was inside my head. Though barely a teenager, I was determined to find my way out, only to find the wrong people in the wrong places. I ventured over into the dark side of life.

Like my mother, I was a virtual prisoner in my own home. I couldn't have friends. I couldn't have sleepovers. And was not allowed to go out. By the time I was sixteen, I was finally allowed to date one boy, only to learn later the reason I was allowed to go out with him is because he supplied my mother with drugs.

On the occasion of my sixteenth birthday, I met my mother's drug dealer.

When you live on the periphery of society, you invariably cultivate a hook-up. A hook-up is someone to share life's day-to-day traumas, and in many cases, a bed. Hook-ups are in the same shape you're in, but they generally have all the answers. They can tell you what's right with the world, and they can tell you why the world is so fucked up.

It makes you wonder how they wound up on the streets in the first place if they have all the answers.

On rare occasions, a hook-up can lead you to a better place, even off the streets altogether. But, in most cases, they take you deeper down the hole you were in when you met them.

That was my first relationship and as it turned out, a fatal one. But it gave me a way out of the hell I was living in, and it gave me my first daughter. Within months, I found myself pregnant. The first thing my parents did when they found out I was pregnant was kick me out of the house, but not without my father getting in a parting shot.

When he learned I was pregnant, he slapped me across the face in anger and proceeded to beat me once again. The fact that I was pregnant meant nothing to him. In fact, he would probably have felt better if he had caused me to have a miscarriage.

When I became pregnant and evicted from my own home, I moved in with the man who would be the father of my baby. We lived with his parents, who had no idea at the time that I was pregnant.

He and I eventually got a place of our own, but by that time I had learned the extent to which he was involved in drugs and our time together became more of a co-existence rather than a relationship.

I was growing more and more pregnant. While I and others around me, especially my mother, knew I was ill-prepared to bring a child into this world, I never considered having an abortion. Given everything I had experienced as a child, I had also developed an unshakeable faith during that time. Now, on the verge of giving birth, my faith remained strong and, against the wishes of many, I never even consider abortion as an option.

By the time my baby was born, I was 18 years old, living with a man I didn't love who was tangled up in the drug world, and having parents who did not want me, but were determined to take my baby.

I realized I was repeating the life of my mother. I was a teenage mother not knowing how to raise a baby, and not even able to support one. My faith is the only reason I held on for that first year. The baby's father and I were living together, but merely co-existing in the same house. He went his way and I went mine. I was fighting my parents to keep my daughter and needed a way to support the two of us.

During my teenage years, I had become a talented dancer and discovered that dancing may be a way to generate income, which took me into some pretty seedy places.

The adult dancing world is an interesting one and has many variations. There are strippers, there are pole dancers, and there are prostitutes who merely disguise themselves as dancers. Even though I could probably make good money doing any of those, I had no interest. I was still a Christian, and despite all I had gone as a child teenager, I had my pride and a set of values.

Within that world of adult dance, however, I discovered a more elegant, classier style of dancing. It was one which interested me and didn't require me to take my clothes off or allow grotesque or disgusting customers to drool on me. I learned that I could put my talents to use as a dancer without being a stripper or a pole dancer.

I found work as a dancer modeling evening wear and bathing suits and blessed to know I could support my baby and me without taking my clothes off. The money was good, and I must admit, I was good at it.

All the while, my parents became more and more disapproving of my lifestyle and inability to take care of a child, and more and more determined to rescue the child, even if it meant resorting to kidnapping. My mother knew only too well from her own experience that I was not giving my child what she needed. That is why she and her husband hatched a plan to take her from me.

I only added fuel to that fire by becoming pregnant again. Two years after the birth of my first daughter, I had a second. After enduring a barrage of assaults and abuse by my mom and her husband, they did exactly what I feared . . . they kidnapped my babies from me.

Now, through all the darkness and turmoil that consumed me from childhood, my salvation was my street smarts, my savvy and my faith. Through the turmoil of a broken, violent home, sexual abuse and teenage childbirths, I never lost that faith in Jesus I had developed as a child. Though I was certainly not living Jesus' teachings, I could feel his presence, especially when I was giving birth to my children.

I never entertained the thought of having abortions, even though I was not prepared to take care of my children myself. I was living a life of torment and the last thing I wanted was for my babies to be subjected to a life on the streets and no stability. I tried to take care of them the best I knew how, all while getting plenty of input from my family and others, as to how to raise them.

Knowing my life was not what I wanted for my children, I gave them up for adoption. In that same spirit of Jesus, I am thankful today that they all grew up happy and well-adjusted, and today still love their mother.

With my children secure and the spirit of God and Jesus still in my heart, I journeyed on . . . into more mystery, more evil and more darkness. All told, I had three children . . . two daughters and a son. They were my biggest and perhaps the only source of pure joy I had ever known in my life. But each having been taken from me and given up for adoption, that was perhaps one of the darkest times in my life. It was through my three children that I experienced the first inkling of the love I was so desperate for. And now, they were gone from me.

Like my mother when I was born, I was a child having children. I had no training, no love and no support structure to have kids. And my three children paid the price. But by virtue of the grace of God, with little help from me or my family, they have found their way.

They were clearly in better surroundings than I could have provided them, and later in life, I would be reconnected to each them. But at the time, I was empty from their absence and began to sink into the world of drugs and self-abuse.

CHAPTER 6

Pursuit of a Dream

NOW IN MY twenties, I was a mother of two daughters and a son, all of which I had given up for adoption. The world around me was filled with violence, mistreatment and abuse. I had no significant love interest, nor any degree of love and support from my family. I had some degree of musical talent and had long harbored a dream of being in the world of music and entertainment.

In part, to pursue that dream, and in part, to get away from the hellhole that was my environment, I decided to act.

That dream became *Baby B Productions*, a music promotion company in the world of hip-hop entertainment. I was now in the music business and pursuing my dream. I moved to multiple cities where the hip-hop scene was jumping, which took me to cities far from my home.

Once I had relocated, I had an interesting start. I met and married a man and to this day, I cannot state a single reason we got married. He had lingering interests elsewhere, and soon, so would I.

I met another man who was the CEO of a musical production company. As we talked, we discovered we shared many of the same tastes in music and had compatible business interests . . . he wanted to produce musical hip-hop artists, and I wanted to promote them. We began to shape what might be considered a 'back of the napkin' business plan, with the objective of collaborating in our mutual interests.

We arranged to meet and discuss the issue further, and as so often happens, our business discussion turned personal. We began to discuss my husband and they status of my marriage. When I told him my husband and I no longer shared a marital bond, he wasted no time in taking advantage of the opening.

I must admit, the feelings were mutual. I fell and fell hard.

We ended up in a hotel room and spent a weekend together. In a very short time, we were expressing our passion and our love for each other. For the first time in my life, I felt true love

I have gone through many relationships in my life and many marriages, including the father of my children, but none of them provoked the same feelings that I had for this man.

The torrent fling we shared that weekend must have been reminiscent of the passionate night my parents shared when I was conceived so many years ago. I felt passion, love, and pure exhilaration, possibly for the first time in my life. I felt I not only had a business partner, but a partner I could share the rest of my life with.

I have known many men in my life . . . men who beat me, men who abused me, men who fathered my children, men who loved me, and men who have betrayed me. But none of them, including this one, gave me anything close to the love I so desperately wanted.

Ultimately, it all comes down to love. It was love that I sought from my father. It was love that I saw from my stepfather. It was love that I sought on the streets. It was love that I sought in all of the wrong places. And it was love that I thought I had finally found in a man whom I loved deeply, and he professed to love me as well. That is, until he betrayed me.

Once he had his hooks in me, I discovered he had elsewhere as well. It soon became apparent that when I thought I was this man's perspective partner, I was merely his latest conquests. I was genuinely in love with this man. And though he told me continuously he had the same feelings, those feelings were not evident in his behaviors. If I was going to make a go of it in the music business, it would not be with him.

I decided to look elsewhere.

Though spread out across thousands of miles, from Atlanta, to Los Angeles, to New York, the music scene is a tight knit community. Songwriters, artists, and producers are collaborating between Nashville, Miami, and Philadelphia.

I eventually looked elsewhere to continue my dream in other locations where I had connections and set up shop there. I had no longer gotten settled in when I got bad news back home.

My stepfather back in Florida had suffered a stroke.

I had to get home and had no way to get there. I resorted to a time tested, but dangerous solution . . . I would hitchhike.

I found my way to a local truck stop and managed to flag down a trucker and tell him my situation. He reminded me that trying to hitchhike from Pennsylvania to Florida would be a risky proposition. He tried to talk me out of it . . . that is until I told him that my father was a truck driver.

Like the music business the community of truck drivers is a close knit one. Every driver knew every other driver, and when I told him who my father was, that changed everything.

"Your father was the *Bear*?' he asked in astonishment? Without hesitating, the driver got on his CB radio and relayed the message to other drivers up and down the East Coast... '*I have the Bear's daughter with me, and she has to be in Florida as soon as possible.*'

That message was the beginning of a series of rides and transfers from one trucker to another, which resulted in me getting home safely in a matter of days. I knew my father had a reputation in the community of truck drivers, but until that relay of rides, I didn't know just how much weight he carried. I was dropped off less than a block from my parent's home.

Now to my stepfather . . . he was in a bad way. He was home from the hospital, but his recuperation was slow. I was once again playing the role of housekeeper and nursemaid to my stepfather, but that did not last long. It was not long before things resorted back to the way they used to be.

In less than two weeks, my mother kicked me out of the house, and I was literally homeless. I mean fleabag hotels and soup kitchen homeless. That lasted over a period of months until I was able to make arrangements with the woman who was the aunt of my children.

I moved into her apartment and was beginning to get on my feet again . . . that is until I experienced the next strange phenomenon in my life. This one more extraordinary than those in the past.

CHAPTER 8

Another World

ANOTHER MONUMENTAL EVENT in my life occurred in April of 2014. One that would be catastrophic in the physical sense but would bring me a mental and emotional clarity that I never had. It was a horrifying time physically, but one that would take me into another world.

I encountered a bizarre series of illnesses, misdiagnoses, medical malpractices and poor treatment, and literally died on a hospital bed. I was revived merely minutes before my family was to 'pull the plug.' But what was a fiasco in the physical and medical sense, brought about a stark realization and understanding of all I had experienced in my lifetime in the spiritual sense.

What follows is two distinct stories woven into one . . . a disastrous journey through the mine field that is our health care system, followed by a spiritual awakening and enlightenment.

While, for legal reasons, I am unable to reveal the names of specific health care facilities or individuals, all that follows is a true characterization of the events which in 2014.

There was a time earlier in my life that I was in a car accident and suffered a pinched nerve in my back, which was misdiagnosed. That failure resulted in me having the most freakish series of incidents in my life, including my own death.

I have come to conclude there must be two different healthcare systems in our country... one for the rich and the politicians who declare 'our healthcare system is the 'finest in the world;' and another for the rest of us. I do not believe any member of Congress or a celebrity would experience what I experienced. I do not believe Donald Trump, or any member of his cabinet would be taken to the emergency room with a life threatening illness, and be summarily dismissed with a prescription for pain medication.

For the rich and famous, we may have the finest healthcare system in the world. But for the rest of us, it's a crap shoot. Whereas one doctor may see us as a human being, another sees us as just another set of forms to fill out. One nurse may genuinely be concerned about what we are experiencing, and another may view us as yet just another in a long line of ailments to contend with before she can go home.

A health system that is overloaded, understaffed, and under-funded, is not 'the finest healthcare system in the world.' I know. What I witnessed, and more painfully what I experienced, took multiple doctors, multiple nurses, and multiple hits and misses, before getting to the right diagnosis and the right treatment. Even then, I literally died.

While I believe the majority of healthcare professionals genuinely care about the quality of their work and the health of their patients, far too many are over loaded and overly reliant on prescription pain medication as a quick fix. While that is not the system of which the rich and famous rely, it is what the rest of us endure on a daily basis.

In a span of ten days, I was transported to three different hospitals by emergency medical technicians. It all began with an increasingly debilitating pain in my neck and down my left arm. The first two hospitals examined me and summarily dismissed me with pain medication that did nothing but exacerbate the situation. The third finally got the right diagnosis and the right treatment, which resulted in surgery, an extended hospital stay and being prescribed months of therapy that my insurance would not cover. In the midst of it all, I flat lined and was declared dead, and barely escaped a permanent demise when I awoke merely minutes before my family was to suspend life support.

What follows is a bizarre and painful ball of confusion, delirium, and life and death experiences, followed by an emerging clarity of the pattern of all the mishaps and catastrophes that dominated my life. For legal reasons, I cannot, and in some cases am unable to reveal the names of individuals, healthcare facilities, or institutions. But the events actually occurred.

I was looking forward to 2014. The year was beginning to trend nicely. I was living with my sister-in-law in a townhome. I had graduated from high school and was making preparations to go to college. My media promotions company was beginning to gain momentum and I was preparing for an upcoming event. I was still dealing with the post-traumatic stress and fibromyalgia that had disabled me all through my childhood and adult years, but I was hoping it was beginning to subside.

My three children, though not with me, were growing to become healthy and happy adults. My oldest daughter was living out-of-state and preparing to be married. My son was also out-of-state but preparing to return to Florida, where he had been accepted to attend college. My third child, who was about to turn twenty at the time, was living close by.

I was in hopes that I was going to be able to put the ugliness and dark shadows that seemed to have been following me since birth, behind me. The beatings, the abuse, the paranormal experiences, and the pain that had dominated my life, I had hoped, were becoming a thing of the past. Little did I know that what awaited me would be the most painful of them all.

What happened next would change me in such profound ways that I would never again be the woman I was. I would never know the ability to walk or function in any way that would be considered normal. The experiences of my childhood and as a young adult were very painful for me, emotionally. I would now know the physical equivalent of those mental and emotional experiences. And, it is only thru God's grace and power that I am even here to tell this story.

In the early part of April of 2014, I began to experience a tingling sensation that seemed to originate in my ex neck and down my left arm to my hand. Assuming I must have slept wrong or lifted something to strain my arm, initially dismissed it, but the sensation did not go away. I was left wondering; did I lift something? Did I do something? Did I move awkwardly to create such a pain? I could not recall anything that I could have done to trigger the pain. All I know is it was a sharp pain and created a tingling sensation and eventually my fingers would go numb.

Over the next couple of days, the feeling persisted. I was still holding out hope that maybe I had slept on my arm wrong because it was acting as if it were asleep. But the pain not only persisted, it was getting worse. Plus, I was beginning to lose my ability to move around freely. I was having difficulty picking things up and raising my arm.

By the third day, the pain was overwhelming. I was in sheer agony. I was bordering on becoming delirious. Either I, or my sister-in-law decided it was much more serious than having slept wrong on my arm, and time to go to the emergency room. One of us called 911. Thus, began my agonizing experience with our healthcare system, and the most debilitating time of my life.

It was Tuesday night, April 15, 2014.

Following the 911 call, emergency medical technicians transported me to what I will refer to as hospital 'A,' sometime between eight and 8:30 PM. I was delivered to the reception nurse at the emergency room. I was put on a stretcher in the questioning began. Only, I was in an increasing state of pain and delirium, and barely able to answer with any degree of coherence. I was able to communicate my name and address and my symptoms. The pain was agonizing, extending from my neck down to my hand.

I was given a battery of examinations and tests, including an EKG. After what seemed like hours of being poked and prodded, all while in excruciating pain, the conclusion was 'there is nothing wrong with your heart.' That was like having a broken leg and being told nothing is wrong with your head. I *knew* nothing was wrong with my heart. It was my arm.

I was in agonizing pain and said to them something is wrong. Just because it's not coming back from my heart there is still something wrong. Why would my neck and arm be doing this if there is nothing wrong?

After a long consultation among themselves I was sent home with the pain being even more intense than when I arrived, with no answers and a prescription for medication that would the t help my situation. So much for the *'finest healthcare system in the world.'*

Round Two

I could not sleep. The pain continued. It became greater. I was having blackouts. The burning and numbing sensation was extending from my left arm all the way down my left leg. It was virtually impossible for me to stand. I could not move. The pain was excruciating. From the time I left Hospital 'A', I was in tears and was bordering on delirium.

I called the first hospital I went to, begging for help, and was told to finish taking my medication. With that, I was hoping that if I did, I would get some relief and be able to sleep. The medication didn't help. I was in a catch 22. I was told not to come back to the hospital until I finished my medication . . . but my medication was having no effect on my symptoms. I'm sure to the hospital staff I just seemed like an out-of-control hypochondriac. But my symptoms were real. The pain was overwhelmingly real. And I'm not sure they believed me or cared. To them, I felt like I was an inconvenience and merely a number, not a patient. Not a human being.

I felt I had to go back to the hospital but was determined not to go back to the same hospital. 911 was once again called and the EMT's responded. The EMT report, in part, read as follows:

> *Patient states her arm is in pain and numb. Patient states pain scale is a 20 on a scale of 1 to 10. Patient has a history of fibromyalgia cardiac and spina bifida.*
>
> *Upon arrival we found a 41-year-old female at her home in a supine position on the ground screaming. Patient states her arm is numb and she cannot feel her pain. It feels like a pinched nerve. Patient was assisted to a stretcher and placed in a semi-prone position (sitting at a 45° angle) and secured for safety reasons.*
>
> *At her request, we transported the patient to Hospital 'B.'*

As the report indicated, this time, at my request, we went to Hospital 'B.' All It was five days after my initial ER visit with Hospital 'A.'

By this time, the pain was beyond anything I had ever experienced. In the sensation had extended from my left side to my right. I was virtually paralyzed. I was screaming uncontrollably and thrashing around the emergency room desperately in search of some relief, and answers. Having lost my mobility, screaming and sobbing was the only way I felt I could get attention from the emergency room staff. I was probably causing a scene in the hospital, but I didn't care. Protocol goes out the window when you are in that much pain.

After the horrible experience I endured the Hospital 'A', I was in hopes the experience would be better and I would get some relief and answers in Hospital 'B'. I was wrong.

Upon arrival at the ER of Hospital 'B', the Emergency Room staff report was as follows:

This is a 41-year-old female presented to the emergency department with a one week history of upper back and neck pain with radiation of numbness and spasm into her left upper extremity. She denies any recent injury, fevers, headaches, or low back pain. Patient is very hysterical in the emergency department and was recently seen at a local hospital, and given a prescription for oxycodone and Flexeril, which she states is not helping. The onset was one week ago, and in the course/duration of symptoms is constant. Location: upper thoracic spine. Type of injury: none. Radiating pain to the upper left extremity. The character of symptoms is pain and loss of mobility. The degree at present is moderate. The exacerbating factor is Tylenol. Associated symptoms: denies headache.

After a battery of examinations, the findings were as follows:

There is no cervical spine fracture or malalignment. The central spinal canal is grossly patent. There are no significant degenerative changes. No gross soft tissue abnormalities. No cervical spine fracture or malalignment.

Once again, in a span of five days, after hours of poking, prodding and tests, I was given a prescription of prednisone, a collection of materials on muscle spasms, some oral instructions, and dismissed.

Round Three

After returning home and feeling no better than I did five days ago when this whole saga began, I was hopeful the new drugs that had been prescribed would help, but was sensing that something bigger was happening inside my body . . . inside my mind too. By this time, I was drifting in and out of consciousness. The pain was overwhelming. There were fleeting moments when it became so intense, I would have what felt like an out-of-body sensation. I could feel the pain, yet I could look down and actually see myself, as if I were observing someone else.

At the time, I couldn't tell if I was just in a state of delirium or experiencing some form of a higher power.

I had always believed in God, but now felt like he was literally inside my body directing my actions. The experiences were fleeting, but very real.

Other than those brief moments, there was no relief. I was back in my apartment and the pain was as intense as ever. Additionally, I had no mobility. And, as opposed to helping, the drugs were making things worse. I was taking the steroid that had been prescribed for me, on top of the cocktail of other drugs I was taking from previous ailments. As much as I had hoped the second hospital would be more helpful, everything physically, mentally, and emotionally was still in a downward spiral.

I was becoming increasingly fearful for my life. I called the hospital and was told once again that I simply needed to let the medicine do its work. The medicine was actually making things worse. I called my mother in search of answers and some guidance. Determined that I not be alone, she had the father of my children come and get me and take me to his house. I was no better, but at least would not be alone.

He took me to his house, and the downward spiral continued. I was in sheer agony and spent most of my time there rolling on the floor in excruciating pain. After two days of being doubled over in pain and screaming uncontrollably, I experienced yet another out-of-body sensation. This time, I was spiritually taken to a place I had never been.

Being around me at that time would have been difficult for anyone. I was in agonizing pain. I could not move. I was in and out of a state of delirium. Nothing gave me relief. During this time, I was immobile or unable to walk or even get off the floor. With things progressively getting worse, I had no alternative but to once again call 911.

In the midst of all of the agony and chaos, I once again drifted into another realm. Instead of being the woman lying on the floor, uncontrollably sobbing, I rose above that woman. For that brief period, that woman was not me, but someone I was observing. The best way I can describe it is I was a spiritual, almost angelic, presence overseeing what was taking place below me.

When the ambulance arrived, my caretaker, assuming I was unable to walk, was going to pick me up and physically carry me into the ambulance. Much to his surprise, on my own, I instead was able to walk. For that brief moment, a higher power once again emerged. For the past two days, I was completely immobile. Yet, for that brief shining moment, I was able to walk unassisted to get into the ambulance.

I and everyone around me was momentarily stunned. The unthinkable had just happened. For more than two days, I was unable to move. I couldn't feed myself or even go to the bathroom by myself. Yet, I was able to get up and walk to the ambulance.

Once I arrived at Hospital #3, I was rushed into my third different emergency room in less than a week. Almost immediately, I could sense something different about this hospital. Like the other two, the medical staff began asking a series of questions. And, like the other two, they began to conduct a series of tests. A, like the other two, I was screaming hysterically in unspeakable pain.

But unlike the other two, I was not summarily dismissed with more prescribed medications. They knew nothing was wrong with my heart. It was my back, just as I had been trying to explain. My back was unable to support my body. The spina bifida and fibromyalgia that I had been living with for years finally caught up with me. The remedy was not prescription medication, they said, but surgery. I would have to have rods inserted into my back to reinforce the support of my neck and shoulders.

In what seemed like a matter of minutes, I was being rolled down the hallway into surgery. As I was being rolled on the gurney, the ceiling lights above me were flashing like strobe lights in a disco. Once we arrived in the operating room, I, again began to have an out of body experience. It was if I were no longer on the table being on the receiving end of the doctor's scalpel, but residing above in some spiritual existence, watching the surgeons do their work.

I observed as they proceeded to operate. I watched the blood ooze from my neck as the surgeons made their initial incisions. Though my physical body was unconscious from the effects of the anesthesia, my spiritual body was being given a bird's eye view of the entire procedure. I yet again was experiencing something beyond my physical being that I could not explain.

When the surgery was completed, I had a T-shaped set of rods in my back to support my back, neck, and shoulders. I awoke in the recovery room with my family looking on. We were told I was not out of the woods yet, and that my recovery would be delicate and arduous, given the complications of my medical history. Thus, began the long road back, and yet another unexplained spiritual occurrence.

At some point during my recovery, my heart stopped beating and the efforts to resuscitate me were to no avail. I was for all intents and purposes, dead. I was placed on life support to preserve my organs. I have no record of how long I was in this state, but it was long enough that the medical staff put forth the issue to my family of 'pulling the plug.' With no indication I could be revived, they agreed. Literally minutes before they were to cease all artificial means of life-support, I miraculously awoke.

Once revived, what lay before me was months of hospitalizations and physical therapy to regain the movement and mobility I once had. What also lay before me was the medical diagnosis that that may never happen. That, however, was in the physical world . . . within the realm of what doctors and therapists could conclude based on the world that they knew. Something, however, was brewing beyond their world. Something, not in the physical existence as we know it, but in the spiritual realm... the world beyond.

While undergoing my recovery, and the medical and legal issues that accompanied that recovery, a pattern started to take shape in my mind. Though there still many unanswered questions, a clarity began to emerge that I never had. Was there some strange connection between all the bizarre occurrences I had experienced over the past forty years? Was there some mystical connection between what, up to now, seemed to be random and tragic events in my life?

Was there some strange, 'other world' connection between the paranormal experiences I endured as a child, the strange tales of guerrilla warfare my father shared with me, and that which I had experienced in the hospital? Why was I subjected to those 'out of body' experiences that I had? Why was I taken into another realm? Could the events that seemed totally random and unconnected in this world, be perfectly logical in that other world?

Exactly what it was, I didn't fully understand. But there was something at work that went far beyond my physical recovery. I was seeing things I never looked for. I was knowing things I had no business knowing. I was being given answers to questions I never asked. I began to see things I never saw before. I began to understand things I never understood before. I began to see things others couldn't see.

The messages I was given by my father so long ago were starting to take shape. They were beginning to make sense . . . about his experiences in Vietnam . . . the testing that was done on human beings . . . the killings . . . him being 'inoculated' . . . him telling me of how I had been inoculated through him, and how I would be 'observed' because of it. There was a strange and eerie pattern that began to fit together . . . him telling me of another world . . . the paranormal experiences I encountered when I was a child . . . the men in the black sedan coming to visit me.

Was I being observed? Was I being protected? Was there a presence beyond this world that I had been entangled in all these years . . . because of my father's doings?

And now, this? Lapsing into a coma and being declared dead . . . only to come back to life moments before they were to pull the plug.

Physically, I was a shell of my former self; unable to walk or do simple tasks without assistance . . . but mentally, I was beginning to connect the dots. What my father shared with me those many years ago no longer sounded like 'other world' gibberish. It began to make sense. I had no bodily strength and no mobility, but my mind was gaining a sense of clarity I had never had.

After my hospitalization, I moved back in with my mom, and began my convalescence alongside my stepfather who was recovering from a stroke. We laid in sofas side-by-side talking and watching television. We discovered that we enjoyed the same TV shows. We also began to develop a closeness we had never before shared.

Possibly out of concern for his own mortality, he became reflective and emotional in ways I had never seen before. He told me he was sorry for all of the things he had done to me. He expressed remorse for not being a better father to me and not helping me more. He felt that many of the things that happened to me could have been avoided if he had been a better father.

As we convalesced together, we became much closer. I concluded that many of the problems we had experienced earlier in our relationship could be traced back to my mother. In many ways, it was my mother that prevented me and my stepfather from becoming closer.

Though it was a difficult time for both of us physically, it was a highly emotional time in the development of my relationship with my stepfather. Many of our conversations brought each of us to tears, and to this day, it is difficult for us to come together without breaking down.

It was during that time that my stepfather truly became my father.

At some point later, maybe months, my parents decided to move out-of-state and take me with them. It was there that I continued my rehabilitation from the hospitalizations and all I had experienced.

My time with them was a time of rehabilitation and I gradually began to regain my strength and was beginning to recover. However, just as I was beginning to regain my strength, my parents decided to move back to their original home.

I had no desire to go back into the hellhole that offered me nothing but abuse, drugs and mistreatment. Besides, I had some unfinished business elsewhere. Both my music and the man I loved were in one of the cities where I had lived, and I needed to find out if I could make a go of it with either of them.

CHAPTER 8

My Stepfather

AFTER MY PARENTS' divorce, my Mom wasted little time before she remarried. My life was a rocky beginning with the man who would become my stepfather, but our relationship would eventually turn into one of mutual love and respect. When he came into my life, I was nine-years- old and living in a world of violence and abuse. I was confused, mistrustful and full of rebellion. He was a man of rules, control and a determination to dominate both my Mom and me. Something had to give.

It was during the time after my hospitalization and after my stepfather's stroke when the two of us convalesced together and became close. That was when I began to view him as my real father.

However, it did not start out that way.

My stepfather came into my world at the most vulnerable time in my life. I had endured physical and sexual abuse from the time I was a toddler. I was living in an existence of rage, abuse, and violence between my mother and father. I had endured an array of paranormal experiences, which no one could or even tried to explain. In addition, I watched my mother and father engage in behaviors, both with each other and with others, that no child should ever witness.

My biological father was an angry, violent man. His only form of parenting was either silence or either dangerous explosions of rage and beatings. He was also a mysterious man, drifting in and out of my mother's life and mine. There were very few positives that could be said for him, either as a husband or as a parent. Nevertheless, he was my Dad and I loved him, and I was not interested in being ordered around by some stranger just because he was the next man in my mother's life.

My relationship with my stepfather began in a very combative fashion. He was the unstoppable force and I was the immovable object.

From the onset, it was a battle of wills. He was a man who assumed control of his new wife and family, and I was a recalcitrant stepdaughter refusing to be controlled by the new man in my mother's life. He may have married my mother but he did not marry me, and I was not going to take directions from him. I had a father and this man was not my father.

Over the years, our relationship began to change. I remained an out-of-control adolescent trying to find my way, but as I veered in and out of trouble and abusive and dysfunctional situations, e soon became the father figure for which I had yearned.

As my own father transitioned into his new life with a new wife and I was dealing with my own issues, my stepfather stepped up. From the continuing struggle I was having, dealing with the paranormal events I had experienced, to the health problems I was having, to the many traumatic issues I suffered as an adolescent, my stepfather stepped in to guide me.

And he brought children into my life. From the time I was a child, I had always dreamed of having brothers and sisters in my life, and with a new stepfather, that happened. I quickly learned, however, that can be a blessing and a curse.

As I was vulnerable and, in some cases, naïve enough to be exploited, I was. While some of my new brothers and sisters became a healthy addition to my life, others brought a continuation of the dysfunction I wanted so desperately to escape. They also introduced me to something else.

Drug use, especially marijuana, was rampant within my new family and even with my own mother. Growing up in this new environment made me more aware of the drug culture, and eventually a user. Life with my new family was like a party gone bad. Drugs, alcohol, neglect and abuse were the norm. If there was any sense of decorum or discipline, it was my new father that instilled it. Sometimes it worked in my favor, sometimes not.

Though I was becoming a teenager and interested in boys, my parents were very strict about me dating. It was only when I was introduced to my mother's drug dealer that I was allowed to date, and that was because it fed her drug habit.

From the beginning, the man who was my mother's drug dealer and was allowed to date me, had one agenda . . . to get in my pants. That's not to say that I didn't share his interest, but I was being a little more reserved about the matter.

Our first sexual encounter (my first; I was sixteen), took place on an occasion when we were in his car and heading home. He kept bringing up the subject of having sex. Knowing we had already passed all the motels along our route and thinking I was safe, I told him, 'The only way you're going to get in my pants is if we pass a motel.' With that, he immediately turned the car around and circled back to the first motel we came to.

I was a virgin no more.

That was just the beginning of my sexual experiences, many of them adventurous. Once we were in the middle of a pasture and discovered by the shotgun toting landowner. Completely naked, we jumped in the car and barely made our escape as gunshots flew overhead.

Those sexual encounters eventually led to my first pregnancy in the biggest confrontation with my mom and new father.

I was an unwed pregnant teenager living in the household with my mom and very strict stepfather. I tried to hide my pregnancy from my parents for as long as I could. And, given their lack of focus on my day-to-day activities, other than being their maid and housekeeper, I probably was able to hide it longer than if they were paying attention to me. But eventually, nature took its course and I could hide it no longer.

Now, I don't know this for a fact, but I am guessing that when most parents discover their teenage daughter is pregnant, they get upset, express their disappointment, and rant and rave about the impact of the lives, but they eventually work with their daughter to decide how to best take care of the new baby.

Not my mother and not my stepfather.

My mother, as usual, left it all up to my stepfather, and his solution was to beat me with a belt and kick me out of the house.

Now I was pregnant and homeless!

With no place else to go, I moved in with my boyfriend at his parent's house, though they too, were unaware I was pregnant at the time. Once they found out, we had to arrange to get an apartment and prepare for our baby as best we could.

By the time I had my baby, a beautiful baby girl, our circumstances were tough, but I was determined to take care of my daughter. First off, I was determined to shield her from the corrupt environment of drugs and violence that I had known. Beyond that, I wanted to give her a life that I had never had.

My mother and stepfather had different plans. They tried everything they could do to take my daughter from me, believing they knew what was best for her. Knowing what I know now, they were probably right, but I resented their attempts to take away from me the first thing in my life that I truly loved.

Their efforts, mostly driven by my stepfather intensified when I was once again pregnant and expecting a second child. Those were difficult days between my stepfather and me.

I was nine years old when my stepfather came into my life and our relationship was combative from the very beginning. I was emotional and dealing with the many issues that had occurred up to that point. I was in an increasingly angry and rebellious state at the time. My mother had a new husband and she was all too willing to give him complete run of the household, which included me. Yet I was still clinging to the memories of my father and not interested in letting a new man tell me what to do.

My stepfather, like my father was a disciplinarian. He demanded to be in control. He did not allow my mother to work and had very specific ideas about the duties of a wife, and about how a daughter should behave. He expected her to take care of him and the household and expected me to be blindly obedient. If there were disciplinary issues to deal with, he would take care of those matters with a belt or the back of his hand. He demanded a clean and orderly household and expected dinner on the table when he came home from work.

Here's the rub . . . my mother was basically lazy!

All of those household chores he expected her to do when he was away, she delegated to me. All those meals he expected to be on the table when he came home, she delegated to me. All those clothes that needed to be washed and all those floors that needed to be scrubbed were delegated to me.

And if there was a dish that was not perfectly clean, or a pot that was not properly scrubbed, or a spec on the floor that had not been removed, I paid the price. More than once, I was beaten and ordered to wash the dishes all over again until they were clean. More than once, I was beaten and had my head showed 2 inches from the floor to see a spec of dirt that I had missed. Anything that was not cleaned properly or not put in the correct place, my mother blamed it on me.

Much of the early friction and turmoil between my stepfather and me can be traced back to my mother. I was the perfect foil. It was only later that my stepfather and I concluded that she was at the center of many of the problems and battles between us.

The only reason I was finally allowed to date and get out of the house was because the boy I was allowed to see was my mother's drug dealer. And when I became pregnant by him, I was once again beaten and evicted from the household. My stepfather was a strict and sometimes brutal taskmaster, and my mother seldom, if ever, stood up to him to defend me. I was a virtual slave in my own home being overseen by a control freak. Becoming pregnant was, in some ways, my way out of my predicament.

After having one child, my mother and stepfather were determined to take my daughter. Having now had a second daughter, they were more determined than ever, even if they had to resort to kidnapping. And that's just what they did.

Whatever you think about the circumstances and the conditions in which I now had two daughters, they had become the centerpiece of my life and I was determined to keep them. Having a child had given me, for the first time in my life, something that I could love and hold onto. However, my parents (my mother and stepfather) had convinced themselves that I was unfit mother raising my daughter's under unfit conditions.

Under illegal and surreptitious circumstances, they kidnapped my two daughters. I had been robbed of the two things in my life that I truly loved and was once again alone.

It was my stepfather who treated me with strict cruelty. It was my stepfather who beat me and evicted me from my home when he discovered I was pregnant. And it was my stepfather who orchestrated the kidnapping of my two daughters. With that kind of initial relationship, it may be hard to believe that I would come to view him very positively, and as my own real father.

That transformation began to occur over the next few years. Our relationship became much better, and the man who had been a cruel disciplinarian in our earlier times together, was now a man I looked to, in some ways more than I did my own mother. Our relationship really came together after the time he had suffered a stroke and I was recovering from my hospitalization.

In 2013, I was out-of-state continuing my pursuit of a musical promotions business when I learned of his stroke. I was so concerned for his health and so desperate to get home to be with him, I wound up hitchhiking, all the way down the Eastern seaboard.

I moved in with my parents (by this time, the man I referred to as my stepfather I truly regarded as my father) to be at his side. That lasted for less than two weeks as I was soon kicked out of the house once again.

For a period of months I was truly homeless, surviving in day shelters and eating in soup kitchens. Unable to be there for my father, I had to now give full attention to my own circumstances. That is when my sister-in-law became my angel of mercy.

She allowed me to move in with her. She not only gave me a place to stay, but was also very supportive of my ideas about the music promotions business. She became my de facto partner and helped me flush out my business plan. About the time we were getting it ready to put it out on the street, is when I began to experience my own health issues. My plans would have to wait.

After my multiple hospitalizations and my revival from my death experience, I began moved back in with my parents. It was then that my relationship with my stepfather was solidified.

He was recovering from his stroke and I was recovering from my multiple hospital stays. We found ourselves convalescing together, watching the same TV shows together, and having deep and genuine father- daughter conversations.

It was then that I saw a side of him that I had never seen before. He was reflective and remorseful of those earlier days our relationship. He apologized for not being a better father to me. He was regretful of many of the decisions he made that shaped my life. He felt that if he had made better decisions, I could have had a better life.

For the first time in my life, instead of a relationship filled with anger and violence, our relationship was now filled with tears and apologies.

He was now and would forever be my true father.

The two of us began to regain our strength when my parents decided to move out-of-state and took me with them. My relationship with my father continued to be positive in my relationship with my mother remained contentious. It was she, my father and I had concluded, who was the source of much of our difficulties in the beginning.

My relationship with my father was now strong enough to withstand the drug induced negative behaviors of my mother.

After a period of time, the two of them decided to move back to their home and assumed that I would go with them. For me, however, their home represented nothing more than the life of drugs, turmoil, and violence I was so desperate to escape. And besides, I had unfinished business elsewhere.

They returned home and I headed back out to revive my business and another man I thought I loved.

CHAPTER 9

The Con Man

I WILL BEGIN THIS chapter by reminding you that I'm using no names in describing the characters in my life. Much of that is to protect their safety. Given the military and mob activities of my father, and the strange occurrences in my own life, I have experienced scrutiny from the time I was a little girl.

From the federal government, to the mob, to local characters in my family's life, who have been known to inflict violence or exact revenge, I remain concerned for their safety and mine.

On the other hand, there are characters reflected in this book that are simply not worthy of being named. They pose no threat to me or my family, but do not deserve mention. Unfortunately, they are a part of my story, but I refuse to acknowledge them by name.

With that said, when I went to pursue my career for the first time, there were two men in my life that I had truly loved . . . my father and my stepfather. In their unique and sometimes twisted ways, both of them provided me guidance, support, and love, and I was truly appreciative.

While there, I wound up being married to another man and living with him. While he was taking care of his business, I was taking care of mine. In fact, we were pretty much leading separate lives while living in the same place.

During the time I was married to him, I met another man who professed to be a CEO of a music production company and expressed interest in my work. Our business relationship became a personal one and I grew to love this man.

He expressed the same feelings for me and I fell for him completely, only to find out I was being played for a fool.

He was a player and I was one of his trophies. But for whatever reason, I loved him anyway. If you ever wanted proof that love is blind, this would give it to you.

All the while, I had remained in a meaningless marriage. After going to the Northeast and hitchhiking back home when I discovered that my father had suffered a stroke, though I was in one place and he was in another, he professed to still love me.

Yet when I wound up in the hospital myself, I never heard from him. Not once! I didn't even receive a card.

After leaving the hospital and moving back in with my mother and stepfather, my relationship with my stepfather had dramatically improved, however the man I had met left many unanswered questions. Though I had not seen him or heard from him, he remained on my mind and in my heart.

When my parents moved out-of-state, I went with them. I was still in recovery from my prolonged hospitalization but I was getting better. I was gaining weight. I was walking better and feeling stronger.

And when they decided to move back home, given my improving health, my continuing dream of being in the entertainment business, and the unfinished business with the man I loved, I decided to return to where he lived.

A relationship that had begun as a mutual business interest, and turned into a passionate affair, ended just as quickly amidst his sordid array of lies, deceptions, shenanigans and swindles.

The man I loved and thought I may spend the rest of my life with turned out to be nothing more than a womanizing con man. He promised the world and delivered nothing. He was a Class A scam artist and turned out to be not very good at that.

He was, as they say in Texas, 'All hat and no cattle.' While I was still there, he continued to engage me and make promises to get together, but there was always a reason he could not. And after I returned my home in Florida, he showed his true colors.

When I endured the traumas of my illness, my emergency room visits, my death, resurrection and extended hospital stay, I never heard a peep from him. The man who continued to profess his love for me and his desire to see me, never found the time to do so during one of the most painful episodes in my life.

Following my eventual release from the hospital in July of 2015, and once I was recovered enough to do so, I wanted to resume my musical career. By this time, I had settled my medical lawsuits and had the finances to invest in my career.

The musical community where I was living was a tight-knit one and word gets around fast. He knew I was back in town and had received a financial settlement. That made him once again, interested in helping me re-ignite my career, and his own greed.

He knew I had money and that gave him another very attractive reason to want to see me. I was leery having been burned by him once before, but he was still in my heart, and I was anxious to give it one more try.

Having gone through years and even decades of mental, physical, and sexual abuse by family members, friends, and total strangers, trust in men did not come easily for me. And this particular man was especially untrustworthy. But he made promise after promise in his attempts to prove to me he was trustworthy. I agreed to try.

We moved in together.

Things started out okay after we moved in together. He was still pursuing his music interest and I was pursuing mine. Given that I had a little money from my settlement, I agree to loan him some money.

It didn't take long for his true colors to emerge once again.

He was seeing other women. He was lying to me. He continued making promises to me and telling me things that I knew were not true. He was the same man that told me how much he loved me when we first met back in 2009. He was the same man who told me how we could build a business together and spend our lives together. He was the same conman, liar and womanizer he had always been.

As much as I had loved him for all of those years, and for as much as he promised how we spend our lives together, I finally realized the man he really was.

I finally moved out, vowing to never speak to this man again.

From the time I was a little girl, I had always dreamt of living a normal life and being truly loved. My life with my father was dominated by anger, turmoil, and violence. I believed the loved me but was too busy dealing with his own anger to show it.

My time with my stepfather was more of the same. He was a man consumed with his only to control, and he too was unable to express his love. It was only after he had suffered a stroke and we were convalescing together that he showed his love for me.

The various men in my life that I was with and even married were relationships dominated by passion, violence, mistrust and abuse. They were not relationships of love.

This man, however, was someone that I truly loved. And on numerous occasions, expressed that same love for me. And on those occasions, I believed him only to be heartbroken and sadly disappointed in the end.

To me, he was a man I wanted to spend a life with. To him, I was merely a piece of ass with money.

If anything, he re-enforced my inability to trust men.

Even after I left him, he continued to express how he was a changed man and wanted to see me again. As the expression goes, 'Fool me once, shame on you. Told me twice, shame on me.' I had seen enough of the man I once loved and had no interest in being burned, yet again, by his lies and deceit.

I refused to see him and despite his numerous claims, I continue to refuse to see him. He is a user and manipulator of the worst kind and I am happy to finally have him help of my life.

There were three men in my life that I truly loved. My father and stepfather were the first two. This man was the third and he used me and discarded me like a worn out shoe.

It took numerous tries before I learned my lesson, but thankfully, he is no more.

CHAPTER 10

My Dad

As I HAD previously written, my father, (a) was a violent and angry man, (b) experienced a sordid and twisted life both in the military and as a civilian, (c) was potentially responsible for many of the strange and bizarre happenings in my life, and (d) was probably the most influential person in my life.

As I said before, my father had already had a very twisted and perplexing life long before I came into the picture. He had been married and had a son whom I never met. He joined the military and had multiple tours in Vietnam, highlighted by classified and possibly illegal assignments that included murder, torture and other 'black ops' missions. While there, he married a Vietnamese woman and had a daughter I've never met.

When he left Vietnam, he left his Vietnamese wife and daughter, but he did not leave the emotional scars of his military experiences. He returned to this country as a civilian to put his 'black ops' skills and propensity for violence to good use in the only way he could . . . the mafia.

Filled with unresolved rage, he met my mother in a bar in Florida and turned a night of passion into a marriage that neither were prepared for, and a child that neither of them wanted.

If there is an answer or a common thread to the twisted turns, bizarre experiences and mysteries of my life, that answer resides somewhere with my father. Writing about my father has been the most difficult task in telling my story. In part, because it is very emotional for me. In part, because his story is the lynchpin to my story. And, in part because the knowledge and insights he shared with me, places me and my family in a constant state of danger.

All that I have experienced, all the episodes, the unnatural and paranormal experiences I have known since the time of my birth, in one way or another link back to him. And all that I know and all the uncanny insights and powers I possess, originated with my father and what he passed on to me.

Growing up as a child, I remember my dad being a man of mystery. From what I have since learned, he had good reason to be. Up until his death in 2004, which has yet to be solved or explained, he dwelled in the darkest shadows of our society, knowing things he shouldn't know and doing things he shouldn't do. Both, while in the military and later as a civilian, he lived in the dark underbelly of those cultures, amidst an underworld of shady characters, villainous assignments, secrecy and violence.

Prior to marrying my Mom, he was in the military serving in Vietnam, fighting for our country. But his battles were not of the variety that were shown on the six o'clock television news each night. The assignments his unit undertook were those our government would just as soon have us not know about. There are tragedies of war. And then there are the unspeakable tragedies that no one ever talks about . . . and very few even know about. That was the nature of my father's experiences in Vietnam.

Much of who I am today and much of what I know, can be traced to my father. The wisdom, the mysterious insights and the unnatural powers he instilled in me has enlightened and empowered me, yet frightens me. To this day, I struggle to piece together the linkage between what my father instilled in me, and what was instilled by a higher power.

This is his story . . . at least what I know of it.

By the time I was eight years-old, after a marriage filled with violence, my parents split up. My Mom and I moved to another town in Florida where it was just the two of us. She held a variety of jobs as a bookkeeper, a waitress, and as a bartender. But the job I most remember is her working for is a dry cleaner.

My only sense of 'normalcy' during that time was provided by my 4th grade teacher. She had a kind and generous heart and gave me my first real glimpse into another world . . . one not consumed with violence and conflict, but one of 'normalcy.' I remember thinking that I would like to live with her.

By this time, my Mom was dating the man who would become her next husband. Though my Mom liked him, and he clearly liked her, my initial tendency was to reject him. He was not my father and I didn't want anyone else to be with my Mom except my father.

My new stepfather and I immediately began to have what I'll call 'boundary issues.' He was the new man in my Mama's life and had a clear set of ground rules he intended to impose on my Mama and me. I was the petulant child with my own ideas. He was not my father and I was hell bent to remind him of that every chance I got. Our relationship was rocky from the start.

I was being bounced back and forth between my mom and my dad. And, despite his anger issues and his propensity for violence, I loved my dad, and was drawn to him. Besides being my dad, there was something unusual about him . . . something almost unexplainable.

He knew things that seemed extraordinary. He had a wisdom about him. There was something in his life experiences that made him seem to be from another world. He just seemed to know things other people didn't know.

For example, when he would help me with my homework, especially math and science, he had a photogenic memory. He taught me how to have the same. He taught me how to see patterns in things that, to other people, would not make sense.

He taught me concepts about how to learn things that only years later would be taught in the school systems. He seemed to be ahead of the curve, both in terms of concepts and technologies. He revealed secrets and knowledge that, at the time, I was too young to fully understand.

I was intrigued by my time with my father, but the times were hampered by the presence of a new woman in his life. Just as my mom had a new man in her life, my dad had a new wife. And, just as my relationship with my new stepfather had gotten off to a rocky start, my relationship with my new step-mother was even worse.

She was extremely possessive of my father and wanted no one intruding in her space with her new husband, especially a curious and feisty step-daughter. She was much younger than my dad, and even though I was a mere child, she was very jealous of the connection I had with my dad.

She was particularly jealous of the stories he would tell me about his time in the Army in Vietnam. It was almost as if she was trying to prevent him from telling secrets that I shouldn't know.

Though I was unable to comprehend the depth and breadth of what he was telling me at the time, what he was sharing with me was unsettling, to say the least. He would share tidbits about his experiences in Vietnam, but there seemed to be more he did not want me to know.

It was as if he thought I was too young, or could be in danger, if he told me everything. He had a large trunk filled with documents and information he did not want me to see. I was always curious about its contents but was forbidden to go near this trunk.

He told me about being a member of 'hit squads', conducting assignments the public would never know about, nor would want to know about them. He told me of being a member of a special unit and being given assignments other units didn't or couldn't handle.

He told me of his unit being exposed to chemicals and how they had to be 'inoculated' to withstand them. He told me of how, because

I shared his DNA, I, too, was inoculated. I was too young to fully grasp what that meant at the time but would learn some years later.

My father was equally evasive about his current circumstances following his time in Vietnam. It was only later that I would come to know his underworld dealings with organized crime. It was only later that I would come to know and appreciate what the word 'syndicate' meant.

It was only later that I would understand his concerns about me knowing too much, and the potential dangers I could face.

At that time, given my young age, my dad's lifestyle was deemed to be too rough and too risky for a young girl to be exposed to. I was taken back to live with my mom and her new husband, though the custody battles continued.

Both of my parents seemed to want me, but I'm not sure if it was because of wanting me, or them not wanting the other to have me. Their custody disputes were not those that would be fought through the court system. They were usually decided by what today, would be considered kidnappings. There were occasions when I would be whisked away by one of my parents without notice or warning.

The result was a childhood that consisted of going back and forth between a mother and stepfather who weren't sure they even wanted me; and a father and stepmother whose lifestyle was deemed to be too dangerous or too risky for me. I had a father and mother who fought over me, and two step-parents that would just as soon me not be in their lives.

As I grew older, I learned more about my father . . . about his time in Vietnam and his life afterwards in organized crime. He had cousins associated with the underworld, and given his military training and background, he would be a perfect fit in the underworld.

The more I learned, the more I began to understand the magnitude of just how mysterious, but how extraordinary his life was. I also began to understand the impact his life had on me and the extraordinary circumstances I had experienced.

As a teenager, I finally had the opportunity to see the contents of that trunk that I was forbidden to see. One day when my father was not paying attention, I snuck into the room where the truck was located and began to go through its contents.

What I saw was both revealing and shocking. I saw gruesome photographs of Vietnamese children. I saw maps of where American POW's were located. I saw documentation revealing the use of mustard gas and other chemicals that were employed during his time in Vietnam.

As I went through the contents of the trunk, I began to piece together information my dad had selectively shared with me when I was a child. I began to understand why he was determined to prevent me from seeing these contents.

I pieced together that he was part of a unit of 'super soldiers', trained to undertake only the most dangerous and secretive assignments by our military. I remember him describing to me how his unit consisted of a group of 'killing machines.' I learned about his military experiences in 'Black Ops' and how he also served as a mercenary.

I learned more about what he meant when he said he had been 'inoculated' to withstand just about anything, and how his inoculation had been passed on to me, and how, as a result, I would be able to withstand anything.

I began to think back to all that he had shared with me when I was a child . . . all the lessons he had taught me; all the things he knew that I don't dare write about. Everything my father taught me and told me about seemed to be shrouded in mystery and the potential danger of knowing too much. He talked about the possibility of him being 'watched' because of the things he knew, and how I too, could be in danger if I was in possession of the same knowledge.

I began to think of the 'paranormal' experiences I had endured as a child and began to wonder if there was any connection. I thought back to the men in the black sedan coming to visit me when playing on the monkey bars after my own experience. I remembered their peculiar line of questions.

I also pieced together more about his life before, during and after Vietnam. Before he went to Vietnam, he had been married once before and had a son, which meant I had another half-brother who was older than me living in the area. I also learned about his marriage to a Vietnamese woman and had a daughter over there; which meant I had another half-sister that pre-dated me, as well.

I had siblings I would probably never know.

I began to see the connection between my father's life in Vietnam and his later life in organized crime. I learned why he was as secretive as he was all these years . . . why he was away from home all those times, working as a 'truck driver.'

He seemed to know way too much about things such as the Kennedy assassination, or the disappearance of James Hoffa. He spoke openly about things not only in Florida, but in places like Las Vegas and New York City.

His life extended far beyond the boundaries of Florida. His universe consisted of an underworld I was just beginning to understand. I felt I was just beginning to unravel the many mysteries of my father's life, and the connections to my own life, when in 2004, he mysteriously died of questionable circumstances.

Like his life, his death was shrouded in a mystery that has yet to be solved. Did his wife, my step-mother, have something to do with his death? Did he know too much? Had he seen something he was not supposed to see? Was she part of a sinister plan to eliminate him?

At the time of his death, I was a teenage mother living in my own underworld. But my father and I had stayed in touch and I had suspicions. I was determined to know more about the circumstances of my father's death, and my step-mother's involvement.

There is so much I could say about my Dad, but that could be another book by itself.

He was a walking paradox. He had a pent-up anger and rage about him, yet he could be as sweet and cuddly as a Teddy bear. He could be rude and abrupt with his friends and family, yet he could charm the pants off a total stranger. He could destroy someone if they crossed him, yet he would turn around and give you the shirt off his back. I was fearful of him, yet I loved him dearly.

He was full of mystery. My dad had an intriguing, mysterious life. And given what I know about him, he had good cause to be mysterious. From his violent upbringing, to his assignments and potential atrocities in the Vietnam war, to his association with the underworld in Florida, he had plenty of reasons to remain mysterious and out of the spotlight.

From those many mysterious experiences, he garnered facts and knowledge about things in this world that the average person will never know. His military assignments in Vietnam exposed him to military and government secrets that have yet to be uncovered to this day.

The most well-known atrocity of the Vietnam war was something called the My Lai massacre, where the U.S. Army sent a battalion into a Vietnamese village called My Lai in search of communist sympathizers. In the process, the troops burned the entire village and slaughtered hundreds of women and children in the process.

My father was assigned to a special military unit that conducted similar assignments that are not known to the public, thus exposing him to many sordid details about how military and governments operate.

From the brutal torture of prisoners, to villages being destroyed, to women and children being slaughtered, my father saw the darkest and most brutal underbelly of war and the extent to which our government will go to win those wars.

During one of his assignments, there was a dogfight with the enemy. And anticipation of the likelihood of being killed, he removed his dog tags and place them on the body of another soldier.

As a result, our government declared him dead and notified his family. When he returned home, his wife had remarried. That was the sequence of events in which he wound up in that bar where he met and married my mom.

While many executed such orders blindly, my father was able to piece together the tactics and strategies our military was employing and cultivate an understanding of things our government hopes the rest of us will never discover.

He saw military and government technologies that were developed in the 1960's and 70's that are just being expose to the general public today.

Years later, when I was 18, I went to visit my dad and discovered a footlocker that contained many of his military records. It also, unfortunately, contained many of those military secrets that he had intended to remain secret. There were maps of underground tunnels and other such documents. He became very upset with me when he discovered that I was browsing through his military files.

Sometime, either during or after his military service in Vietnam, he married a Vietnamese woman and had a daughter by that marriage. This was obviously before I was born, so I don't know if he intended to stay in Vietnam or return to the U.S.

Whatever his intentions, he did return to the U.S. and the rest is history, leaving behind a Vietnamese wife and daughter. So, beyond his many other mysteries, I have a half- sister in Vietnam that I have never met.

When he returned to the U.S. and met and married my mom, his mystery life continued. His extended, unexplained absences when I was a child, were attributed to his work as a truck driver. What was not spoken about were his activities with the Florida underworld.

My father maintained a strict 'Don't ask, don't tell' policy in our house, and any violation of that policy resulted in violence or rage.

I am sure that many of the arguments in battles that took place between my mom and my dad were a result of her being a little too curious or inquisitive about his secretive activities.

Of all my father's mysteries about his life, the ultimate mystery was his own death in 2004.

Whatever happened to him and whomever was involved remains a mystery to this day. It also remains one of the few items on my bucket list to find his killer or killers and hold them accountable. His on again, off again relationship with his second (or 3rd or 4th?) wife, she knows who she is, will be the first place to go to solve that mystery.

Whether directly or indirectly, she was involved with his death and conveniently arranged to have his body disposed of before the authorities could conduct a proper investigation.

When my dad eventually retired in 2003, his wife had to go to work and get a real job. This was not to her liking. And whether it was that, or a combination of circumstances, the two of them divorced.

Later, my dad had to have surgery which was successful, and he was doing well during his recovery.

Unfortunately, sometime following his surgery, my dad and his ex-wife began seeing each other again. He had regained his health but was once again back in the clutches of his 'Delilah.'

The two of them re-married.

Virtually overnight, she had control of all his possessions . . . his private military records, his cache of weapons including an AR15 rifle, his home, his vehicles, his finances, and his storage chest of Vietnam-era files and materials.

A week later, my father was dead.

His wife claimed that he accidentally electrocuted himself while performing some routine maintenance on the house. First of all, my father was a skilled electrician and was very careful when it came to any issue of electrical repairs. Secondly, bruise marks were discovered on his neck that matched perfectly with a cattle prong device.

Additionally, there was no autopsy performed on his body and he was conveniently cremated within 48 hours after his death.

Whether it was the mob, a biker gang, or individuals conspiring to kill him for money, his wife, my overly suspicious and jealous stepmother, was involved in some fashion. That, I know to be true.

At my father's funeral, I could not suppress my anger.

In no uncertain terms, I said, *'I don't know which one of you son of a bitches murdered my father. But I will find out and make sure that you are held accountable, if it is the last thing I ever do.'*

My dad's mysterious life and equally mysterious death will remain with me for the rest of my life. But the ultimate memories I will have about my father, is his extraordinary and uncanny wisdom and what he passed on to me.

His experiences and knowledge of how this world works defy conventional wisdom, and I believe, the key to the extraordinary experiences in my own life. Further, I believe it is time in Vietnam subjected him to various chemicals which were passed on to me through his DNA. There are simply too many unexplained coincidences that tie his life and my own together.

During his time in Vietnam, he clearly saw things he was not supposed to see. As a result, he was under constant scrutiny by the government, even after he returned home. As a direct descendant who shared his DNA, and someone who may have been told secret information, that scrutiny seemed to carry over to me.

When I endured the strange experiences when I was seven, my father was inexplicably stopped in his tracks. The following day when I was on the playground and observed the unexplained object overhead, government officials seemed to know exactly where I was and how to locate and question me within minutes.

There have been multiple occasions, both then and now, in which military helicopters cover over my location.

In the years before my father's death, he told me of world events that would occur years before they actually happened. He told me of government takeovers, military coups, and secret operations that would be exposed. He obviously knew things the government would prefer he not know, and how strange, seemingly unrelated events, were connected. In so many ways, my father taught me the ways of the world . . . from who to look out for, who to trust, and how to take care of myself.

In a normal setting, it would be easy to accuse my father, and by extension me, of being paranoid. But when so many of the things he told me would occur, *do* occur, it's not paranoia.

Given his many flaws, his questionable actions and morality, his mistreatment of my mother and me, his violent behavior and mysterious ways, it would be easy to hate my dad. But the fact is, I love my dad and miss him every day.

My most significant memories of him are not his violent behavior, his brutal treatment of my mother, his stalking or kidnapping attempts of me as a little girl, and not even the mysterious way in which died. My most significant memories are the times we enjoyed being together. I remember those Sunday afternoon drives with he and my mother. I remember the times he would take me to his home in Ocala to go fishing.

He also was the inspiration for the name of my music business. All the time when I was a girl, he used to remind me of the Army expression, "Be all you can be', and called me 'Baby Begonia.' At the time, I thought it was just a reference to my nickname, and only later learned the reference to his army indoctrination. In his honor, I named my company, *Baby B. Productions.*

I remember as a little girl, looking forward to when he would come home from one of his long trips and hold me in his arms.

I love you Dad, and always will.

CHAPTER 11

My Mom

IN THE MANY stories of sordid and twisted lives, my mother's story is one of misfortune, self-indulgence and the desperate need to survive, no matter what the cost nor who it hurt.

As I previously wrote, she never had a chance. She was born into a virtual sewer of white trash. She killed her grandfather and attempted to kill herself before she was ten and was thrust into the role of taking care of her brothers and sisters when she was fifteen.

She wanted out of the life she was living in the worse way, even if she had to marry a man she barely knew to escape. By the time she met and married my father, she was already married, but that seemed not to matter. If the neighbor's grass looked greener, she went for it, legal or not. Having been in the midst of one failed marriage, she pursued another, and was just as equally prepared, much less taking care of a child. She and my father never wanted me and were certainly not equipped to raise me.

Though she caused me great pain and torment throughout my life, through it all, I loved my mother and cared for her in her darkest days. She just never gave herself nor me a chance to experience the good side of life. She never had a chance to experience the joy of true love. Her version of love was a zero-sum game . . . if she loved her husband; she could not love her daughter. One of the two had to give, and it was usually me that was cast aside.

In pursuit of her own love, she subjected me to the worse forms of physical and sexual abuse and seemed to be indifferent to it all. Consumed with her own needs and desires, I remained a distant afterthought. She farmed me out to anyone who would take, which in many cases led to me being raped and abused, even as an infant.

I struggle to love her or have empathy for what she endured as a child, and yet hold her accountable for the many misdeeds that led to my own misfortunes. Knowing what I know, now being a mother and a grandmother, the maternal instinct is a powerful one. Perhaps one of the most, if not *the* most powerful instinct in the universe of nature. Yet, time after time, from my infancy up to her dying days, when given a choice, she chose her needs over that of her daughter.

With my father, she completely abdicated her role as a protector, allowing him to savagely beat me for the most trivial of offenses. In between marriages, she looked to farm me out to anyone to give her the opportunity to roam freely in search of love, lust or excitement.

With my stepfather, she found ways to sabotage any opportunity for us to develop a bonding relationship. During the time I was a budding teenager, she held me in virtual slavery to take care of the household duties her husband expected of her. And when I failed to meet his expectations, she allowed me to suffer the brunt of his wrath with beatings or worse.

All the times I was being molested by my stepsiblings or other family members, she turned a blind eye. My whereabouts were under the tightest of scrutiny. I was only allowed to date when my mother's drug dealer showed an interest in me. That way, she thought, she could keep both of us within reach when she needed us.

From the very beginning, she was too deeply engaged in the pursuit of her own needs, and I was evidently too much of a bother.

It was only during our time in Tennessee, after my hospitalizations and after my stepfather's stroke, that the two of us came to any sort of understanding. She was on my case about something, and I had had enough. Rather than take it, as I had all those years, I confronted her.

I told her in no uncertain terms, '*Your life has been nothing but greed, selfishness and self-indulgence, and I have had enough! Don't you ever come at me again, or I will take you out!*'

She got the message.

In the spring of 2018, my mom's health had begun to spiral downhill fast. She had been hospitalized and though her health continued to decline, she was deemed well enough to rest at home. My stepfather took her back into what would have to be considered a hellhole.

Their trailer was almost hot enough to be uninhabitable. My stepfather was still recovering from his stroke. My stepsiblings were hovering around, doing drugs and leaching off the two of them. And, my mother continued to decline.

I was out-of-state but felt the need to go home and take care of my mother. Ironically, it was also the time I was awaiting the birth of my first grandchild.

I was reluctant to return to my hometown, not because of my mother but because of the horrific environment she was in. With my stepsiblings doing drugs and running roughshod over my parents, the house was not safe, much less an environment for my mom to spend her final days.

Despite my reluctance, my next few weeks were spent going roundtrip between where I was currently living and my hometown where my mom was located. She was in a hellish environment and there was no one there to care for her. I had to take ecstasy just to cope. The situation was so bad, my stepfather threatened to kill himself.

I became my mother's caregiver. I had to administer her morphine. I had to change her diapers. I had to pry her jaws open just to feed her. She could no longer speak. Essentially, I was watching my mother die.

She was fighting for her life, but it was killing everyone around her, including me. Eventually, I told her just to let go! I told her I loved her, and she mouthed I love you, too. On that final night, a priest was summoned but my mom was unable to speak. I wondered to myself if God had ever redeemed her and forgiven her of her sins.

My mother passed away Easter Sunday, 2018, the same day my granddaughter was born.

My grandmother passed away at the age of forty-six, and now my mother passed away at the same age, both of aneurisms. To take the irony further, I was the same age, 46, and amazingly, I'm still here.

As soon as my mother died, my siblings had my stepfather committed to an institution for being emotionally unstable. There is no question my father was suffering all through this ordeal. But this was just a convenient way for my siblings to take control of each of my parent's belongings. For me, the ordeal was the end of a long and painful existence with both my parents.

When I said goodbye to my Mom, I had to say goodbye to my stepfather. I no longer had the emotional strength or stamina to endure anymore pain from either of them. Besides, I had a new granddaughter to focus on.

With no time to grieve, I returned to my home with my sites fully focused on the future and a new grandbaby.

As the sun sets in the west and another rises in the east.

CHAPTER 12

Redemption

WHEN I GOT home from dealing with the death of my mother, I found my house trashed. The same man whom I once loved and I thought would be a part of my future, I no longer loved and no longer had any illusions about the two of us being together.

But he continued to come around. He knew how I once felt about him and was hoping he could still take advantage of me the way he once did. Back then, I was easy prey to him. But no more.

While I was back caring for my dying mother, he was in my home, trashing my house. When I returned home, not only was my house in a total wreck. So was I.

To cope with the death of my mother, the institutionalizing of my stepfather, and the atrocious behavior of my siblings in the midst of it all, I was jacked up on Xanax. I had so much to deal with and no time to grieve.

Life was still happening around me and much of it was chaotic and dysfunctional. From my siblings accusing me of stealing items I had bought, to the trashing of my house where I lived. It was a sad, chaotic time.

But in the midst of the chaos, there was beauty.

I still had my faith. Through everything I had endured, it had never wavered. I learned from the teachings of Jesus, *When a door closes, another one opens*. And it did big time!

On the same day my mother died, Easter Sunday, 2018, my first granddaughter was born. She was my golden light amidst the darkness.

In writing this book, I was advised not to give any names, for the benefit of others safety and because of the legal issue of someone wanting to sue me for slander. I haven't mentioned either of my parents by name, nor my step-parents. I haven't even mentioned the names of my three children to protect their safety. And staying true to that principle, as much as I've wanted to cite my children by name and my granddaughter, I have resisted.

But through everything I've endured ... the sexual abuse, the mistreatment, and the strange, unanswered occurrences I've experienced ... the birth of my granddaughter has come to symbolize my own rebirth.

My three children, though separated from me at an early time in their lives, have been my foundation all of these years. Next to my faith, they have been an extraordinary source of support. Through much of those years, I was probably too consumed with my own issues to properly thank them or show my appreciation for their willingness to stand by me.

I think the birth of my granddaughter brought it all together. In many ways, she has come to embody that nucleus of support that has been so vital to me. When I think of her, I think of my daughter. When I think of my daughter, I think of my other two children. Collectively, they provide the unconditional love I have yearned for all of my life.

No matter how bizarre, twisted or tragic someone's life may be, there has to be some form of redemption to be found somewhere. My redemption came in the form of my three children, and in the form of my first grandchild.

My three children, two daughters and a son, were all given up for adoption and all three today are normal, well-adjusted adults, and more importantly, well-adjusted and productive adults.

Staying with my precedent that I established at the onset of writing this book, I will not reveal the names of my three children. I do not want them to be subjected to any spillover from what I experienced in my own life, nor do I want them to be subjected to any risks associated with my story. So, I will let my granddaughter serve as the exception to symbolize the four of them.

Like so much of my own life, she was not born without complications. She has health issues she must overcome. The difference from my own childhood experience, however, is that she is confronting her issues in an environment of love and care, not neglect and abuse.

My granddaughter was nine pounds at birth and in many ways is the reincarnation of my Mom. She came into this world as my Mom was going out and embodies my mom's spiritual presence as if she never left. Perhaps I am at an age and out of the dysfunctional environments that haunted me all these years, but it is my granddaughter that gives me a sense of normalcy I never had. Through her, I've come to believe I can do things and accomplish things like never before.

I feel like I can take care of the world.

As she is approaching her first birthday, my granddaughter looks more and more like her father. She is sitting up. She is feeding herself and is exhibiting the intelligence of a bright, perceptive child.

To my son and two daughters, I thank you more than I can express for staying with me all these years; and for growing up to become responsible, contributing adults.

To my granddaughter, I never want you to know any of the traumas and mysteries I went through. I want you to continue to grow, remain healthy and embrace the future you have instilled in me.

With your spirit in my heart, I can go forward in continual pursuit of my dreams, and continue seeking answers to the mysteries that have plagued me all these years.

Through you, symbolizing the pride and joy I feel for you and my three children, I have more reason to fight. More reason to put those mysteries to rest. More reason to move beyond the dysfunction and violence that has marred my life.

My life is no longer my own. I have purpose. I still have questions, but I have a reason to pursue them. The things I once tolerated, I tolerate no more. The people I once allowed into my life who are selfish or want to do me harm or take advantage of me, I allow in no more.

The bitterness I once felt, toward my Dad, my Mom, my step-parents and my siblings, I feel no more. Those who remain will continue be the people they are, but they will no longer be those things in my life. Those who have taken advantage of me will no longer be able to do so. I will no longer give them the satisfaction of my anger or bitterness. They do not warrant such and I have moved beyond them.

I have a new purpose and sense of peace I have never felt before. I have many unanswered questions, but I now pursue the answers in peace.

Thank you to my children. I love you and am so proud of you.

And thank you to my granddaughter. You are the symbol of all that lies before us.

CHAPTER 13

Unanswered Questions

A FTER MY MOTHER'S death, I had to come to grips with a lot of truths. Most of all, I had to come to grips with me. Approaching fifty years old, my life had come nowhere close to the way I had hoped. I had experienced as much in my life that many people will never believe. I was angry with the world and I had to find peace... somewhere, somehow.

Fortunately, my Granddaughter and the continued support I received from my children provided that.

I was born a sensitive, caring, generous child. How much of that was a part of my DNA and how much of that was a part of the environment I was living in, I'm not sure. I simply know that from my earliest days as a small child, I was sensitive to what others were going through.

I can remember when I was a child and my mother and father were fighting, and rather than being angered by the rage and violence that I witnessed, I felt bad for them.

The paranormal experiences I endured seemed to accentuate my feelings for others even more. I was able to not only empathize with the feelings of others, I could actually 'feel' their pain. Even animals that I actually stepped on or hurt in some fashion, I could actually feel it.

I'm sure a large part of it was all the rage, violence, and abuse I endured all those years, beginning when I was a little girl. Even then, I just wanted everyone to get along and be nice to each other. Even then, I was just a romantic idealist. Between my earliest readings of the Bible and brief glimpses I had of what a normal childhood looked like, I developed an almost Pollyannish view of how the world should be. At heart, I'm still that little girl.

I felt bad for what my mother was enduring, and I remember wondering why my father was so angry and violent with her. Given what the two of them put me through as a child and what I endured as an adult, I should be raging with bitterness and resentment. Instead, I feel bad for what must have been going on inside of each of them.

Even as those things were occurring, I don't remember feeling angry. I remember feeling mostly fear and uncertainty. It was like I never knew what was going to happen next.

Even the times when I was being molested as a child, I don't remember being angry. Again, fear and uncertainty were the dominant feelings, along with resignation. I was powerless to do anything about what was happening to me, so I remember having the feeling; this is just what it is! I did not know the word at the time, but the predominant sensation I was feeling was empathy.

Later in life, when I was undergoing the agony of my back pains and experienced the sensation of dying and being revived, my sense of empathy intensified. I was determined to recover and at times, I am sure I was a very difficult patient to deal with during that recovery. I'm sure there are people in the hospitals who were dealing with me at the time that would describe me as an absolute bitch!

However, through it all, my heart remained pure.

All through the physical problems I had, the spina bifida, the neck injury, combined with the PTSD in the many heartaches I suffered, I still wanted what was best for everyone. Even those that inflicted pain on me.

In my worst moments, paranormal experiences, the abuse, the beatings, the hospitalizations, my death and revival, I was able to experience an out of body sensation, in which I could observe the event as if it were not me. Perhaps, that was my coping mechanism that allowed me to endure those events. Or perhaps it was a function of the supernatural or spiritual state I was able to attain which was tied to so many events in my life.

As the saying goes, 'I was *in* it but not *of* it.'

One thing has changed, however.

Throughout my entire life, I not only tolerated the negativity around me. Much of it, I had no control over, such as the violence rage and abuse I had been subjected to since infancy. In some cases, I invited that negativity into my life. I allowed many friends, acquaintances and even family members into my life who were filled with nothing but negativity, deceit and destruction. They had no interests other than themselves. They would lie, cheat, steal, and create chaos, and I allowed myself to be around it.

But no more.

If there was a positive benefit from the collection of strange, paranormal experiences, or other bizarre events that occurred over the course of my life, it was that I developed a heightened awareness and sensitivity. I could visibly see the aura surrounding individuals around me. I could see those that were positive, and I could see those that were negative.

I could tell who had my genuine interests at heart, and I could tell who had their own selfish agenda. They did not have to say a word. I could see and feel their energy field and could sense instantly if it was positive or negative. It was almost eerie.

The benefit is that I was no longer tolerant of that negativity nor the negative people in my life. There are people around me who want to do me harm or steal my money. At one time in my life I would have allowed them to be around me. I no longer will.

The paranormal experiences of my childhood also obviously

changed me. The experiences changed me when they happened but at the time, I was too young to understand or act on those changes. I was seven when I had my first experience. Whatever that was, I didn't understand it. And the bizarre experience the following day was no different. Playing on the monkey bars and seeing this metallic object in the sky. It was so close to me I could almost touch it.

And the visit from those government men, and the strange questions they asked me. I didn't understand any of it. I only remember thinking why are they asking me these questions? And about hanging upside down playing bats, of all things. I just remember them being very official looking and driving a big black car.

My death while in the hospital years later, and my recovery from that experience also had an effect on me. I was already a very spiritual person but life after death will change anyone, spiritual or not. My dealings with God after my death became far different and far more intense.

He allowed me to see things I had never seen before. He allowed me to escape my body and observe my behaviors and the behaviors of others as I had never observed before.

He spoke to me in ways I had never heard before. He allowed me to see people, both dead and alive, as I had never seen them before.

He showed me flashbacks of my past life. He showed me how I treated others and how others treated me.

He allowed me to see things in the future. Many of the things he allowed me to see have already occurred, just as he showed me. From the hurricanes, the floods, the volcanoes, the earthquakes and the pending civil unrest that will occur in this country. Much of which has already occurred or in the process of occurring; and much has yet to occur.

At the time, I did not know if I was given a gift or a curse. People talk about ESP, or extrasensory perception. I don't claim to have ESP, I simply know what I know and what I can see.

All I know is there is much unrest and instability that awaits us.

Both within and outside of this country, there are both natural, civil and political events in our future that frightened me. And all I can do is call attention to those events as I see them.

As an individual, all I can do is separate myself from the negativity that has been so much a part of my life, and only allow that which is wholesome and positive to be a part of my life.

My family members who enacted violence against me know their behaviors were wrong and know I will have nothing more to do with their dysfunctional behavior. My parents and stepparents knew the error of their way and apologized for their behaviors. That is no longer a part of my life.

Those family numbers and acquaintances who abused me from infancy to adulthood know who they are, know what they did, and know they are no longer allowed in my life. Their behaviors were sadistic, violent and criminal. If they have not already repented for what they did to me, can only await a judgement far more cruel than I could inflict.

Those who attempted to steal from or take advantage of me and my family members, and they know they are, await their judgment as well. From the man who professed to love me yet only wanted my money to the family members who stole from my parents as they lay on their deathbeds, there's will be a hell not known on this earth.

I say these things not just because I am a deeply spiritual person, which I am, but also because these are mere samplings of things I can actually see.

While for whatever reason I have been given this ability to see things, by no means do I profess to see all. I still have many questions about the numerous strange and supernatural occurrences that have happened in my life. Seeking answers to those questions has been one of my major reasons for writing this book.

I know there is a reason I was born to two parents who were ill prepared, nor even interested, in raising a daughter . . . a mother who was escaping her on version of hell; and a father who injected me through his DNA, with a collection of unnatural wisdoms and understandings from a brutal war in a far-off land.

I know there is a reason I was able to endure the childhood sexual and physical abuses I experienced, and still survive.

I know there is a reason I was given the ability to read at such a young age, and exposed to the spiritual teachings of the Bible, all while residing in a living hell.

I know there is a reason I was exposed to a series of supernatural, paranormal experiences at the age of seven that have remained with me through the entirety of my life.

I know there is a reason I grew up in an environment filled with rage, dysfunction and violence, yet was able to give birth to three beautiful children while only a child myself. I know there is a reason I experienced an illness and series of surgeries and malpractices, which led to my death, only to be revived and with an uncanny ability to see things and know of things to come.

I know these things, but I have yet to connect these things.

I know there is a connection to the universe around us that is at the core of the. I know God and the teachings of Jesus are also at its center.

I know my father's experiences in Vietnam and the underworld are a part of it. I know he was in places and doing things the government would not want us to know. I know that through his DNA and the things he shared with me before his death in some ways subject me to the same scrutiny he experienced.

How is it that I know about floods, volcanoes or hurricanes that are going to happen before they happen? How is it that I know about civil unrest that happens in this country and in countries that I cannot even pronounce, before they happen?

Why is it that military helicopters hover over my residence for an extended length of time?

Given all I have experienced, from the violent surroundings of my childhood, the paranormal experiences, my death and revival, and all else that has consumed my life, I should be a bitter, resentful woman. Instead, I remain generous to a fault.

God has given me an energy and He's not finished with me yet. He has made it clear there is more to do, but not until I regain my full ability to walk. I don't dare ask what those things are, but I wait.

The questions remain. And fortunately, so does the heart.

Epilogue

FROM THE VERY beginning, I had an intuitive sense that mine would not be a life of the contentment and love that all little girls wish for. When I was born the only child resulting from a passionate, but tumultuous relationship that Florida bar, my life would not be one of normalcy, but of the truly bazaar.

I had the first of the many strange and bizarre incidents in my life happened on the occurrence of my seventh birthday, and I was subjected to an out-of-body paranormal experience that few people on this earth have ever known, and what even fewer have actually been willing to talk about.

Having survived the strange ordeal, I did what any seven-year-old girl would do... I tried to find some sense of normalcy and stability. My efforts were undermined by the turmoil that was taking place between my parents. When my mother took on a new husband, and a stint with my grandmother, I felt some relief . . . although only temporarily.

The bizarre experience left me confused, angry and in search of answers. Getting none, and worse, being dismissed as a child with an overactive imagination, I grew angrier and more rebellious. I was just old enough to venture out into the world, but not yet wise enough to know better. The results were predictable.

Following the death of my grandmother, I looked for my escape path. Though barely a teenager, I was determined to find my way, only to find the wrong people in the wrong places. I ventured further into the dark side of life.

The darkness continued. Though a mere child myself, I now had a daughter. As a young mother, I had to battle my own parents in my efforts to keep my daughter, all while in search of sanity.

A second monumental moment of the bizarre, occurred in 2014, when I died on a hospital bed and amazingly came back to life. It was a result of a series of illnesses, misdiagnoses, medical malpractices, and ultimately divine intervention. I was taken from my body and able to see myself in an almost angelic position.

After recovering from my life-death-back to life ordeal, I moved back home with my mother. By then, I was a little older and a little wiser, and I began to learn the true story of my father. For the first time, I learned of the dark secrets of his life in Vietnam, and the secrets our Government never wanted us to know.

Between the surreal experience at the age of 7, my death on a hospital bed, my resurrection, and the dark secrets of my father's military history, I found myself in possession of facts I shouldn't know; and powers I shouldn't have. My life became a constant existence of what many would call the occult or just plain spooky.

When you strip away all the strange and bizarre happenings in my life, underneath it all was a love of music and a desire to produce. With the means and the determination to escape the macabre life I had been living, I took off in pursuit of my dreams.

When things weren't happening there exactly the way I wanted, I pursued another hotbed of hip-hop and world of music. But my step-father's stroke cut that short. I headed back to be with him, hitchhiking all the way.

After my step-father's stroke and the horrendous circumstances with my mother and step-siblings back in Florida, I once again headed back to my home. As my mother's health declined, I embarked on a series of round-robin trips between my home and Florida where my mother was. In the midst of turmoil, greed and mystery with my step-siblings, I had to get away from their madness. I said my final good-byes to my mother.

In the sunrise-sunset experience of birth and death, weeks after the death of my mother, I welcomed the birth of my first granddaughter. Though many questions and mysteries remained, I found a renewed sense of self.

In the midst of it all . . . the extraordinary experience on my seventh birthday . . . my experience with death and revival . . . my father's story of secrets and black ops in Vietnam . . . the strange powers that have been injected into my body . . . why me? Why was I given a life not of a normal person, but of a woman in possession of a strange gift? Or curse? Why?

The questions remain and the search for answers continue.

As I approach my fifth decade of being on this earth, I reflect on the many aspects of my life . . . my tumultuous upbringing, the bizarre and supernatural experiences I have had, the abuses I was subjected to from the very beginning of my life, the dysfunction of my family, my illnesses, my death, my rebirth, and ultimately my very survival.

My father was mysteriously killed in 2004 and I hold to this day my determination to sort out the events of his death and confront his killer or killers. Survival skills I inherited, I inherited from him. Ironically, he was the source of much of my childhood abuse but was also my teacher and mentor for how to endure and counter that abuse. The skills he learned in the military were the same skills he tried to instill in me.

I am eternally grateful for the time we had prior to his death in which I was able to partially connect the dots between his life and mine, and many other mysteries of the knowledge and power be bestowed upon me. Though we lived together for only partial and intermittent times, he remained a central force to who I am.

My stepfather was also an integral part of my life. Though we had a very rocky beginning to our experience together. I was subjected to physical and sexual abuse, but he eventually became the father that gave me a sense of structure and support.

His debilitating stroke, which occurred when I was living in the Northeast, is the reason I suspended my professional pursuits and returned home at the time. We became close and in many respects, I view him as my real father.

Though he is still alive as of this writing, for my own sanity, when my mother died, I had to view my father as being dead also. I had to say goodbye to him when I said goodbye to my mother. His children, living lives of drugs and abuse, are bad news in so many ways and were controlling his life at the time. For my own protection, I couldn't allow myself to go back into that environment.

My mother was perhaps the most tragic, complex, and paradoxical figures in my life. Much of our time together was characterized by disagreements, turmoil, confrontations, and abject indifference to my plights. In many circumstances, she made choices that were detrimental to me, her own flesh and blood, in favor of individuals that should have meant far less to her. It was only in the latter stages of her life, when her death was imminent, that we found a place of forgiveness and caring for each other.

In those final days, I returned home to care for her, which afforded us the opportunity to say many of the things that needed to be said. As I fed her, gave her medication, and changed her diapers and linens, she revealed some things to me that I had long suspected, and I shared with her what I experienced on the receiving end of her motherhood.

In the waning days of her life, combined with the pending birth of her great grandchild, we were able to find peace in a setting in which little could be found.

When she was brought home from the hospital for the final time, instead of being taken to a hospice that would provide her a comfortable and caring place in which to live her final days, instead she was taken back to a trailer which was uncomfortable and filled with more dysfunction. Her remaining stepchildren which instead of caring for her, were more preoccupied with their own selfish lifestyle.

It was in that uncomfortable and uncaring environment that my mother and I were able to embrace each other . . . to forgive each other.

Now, with the death of my mother, the birth of my granddaughter, and having said goodbye to the turmoil, abuse and dysfunction that has been at the core of my existence, I once again look to the skies.

Though this time, I don't look for redemption . . . God has granted me that. I simply look for answers . . .

Why Do these things happen to me?
What are these powers?
What do I do with them?

It is those answers that will be my ultimate peace.

*   *   *